D0919444

Beyond Metabolism:

The New Japanese Architecture

Michael Franklin Ross, AIA

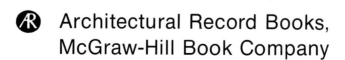 Architectural Record Books,
McGraw-Hill Book Company

New York	Auckland	Johannesburg	Montreal	Paris	Tokyo
St. Louis	Bogotá	London	New Delhi	São Paulo	Toronto
San Francisco	Düsseldorf	Madrid	Panama	Singapore	
		Mexico		Sydney	

Acknowledgments

The research for this book was made possible in part by a Fulbright-Hayes Fellowship for Independent Research. I am indebted to the United States Educational Commission in Japan for awarding me the Fellowship and thereby affording me the opportunity to conduct what I believe to be a comprehensive survey of Japan's current architecture and urban design. I wish to thank all the members of the USEC/Japan, especially the Honorable Robert S. Ingersoll, Ambassador to Japan, Mr. Alan Carter, Chairman, and Mr. Samuel Jameson, as well as Mr. John Barnett and Caroline Atsuko Yang, both of whom served as Executive Secretary.

This book is dedicated to Anna Hisoo Han, whose unstinting support, encouragement and strength prevailed throughout the research, writing and production of this small addition to the recorded history of Japanese architecture.

M. F. R.

Published by Architectural Record,
A McGraw-Hill Publication,
1221 Avenue of the Americas,
New York, New York 10020

Library of Congress Cataloging in Publication Data

Ross, Michael Franklin,   (date)
Beyond metabolism.

(A McGraw-Hill publication)
Includes index.
1. Architecture—Japan.
2. Architecture, Modern—20th century—Japan.
3. Metabolism in architecture (Movement)
I. Title.
NA1555.R67   722'.1   77-13696
ISBN 0-07-053893-X

The editors for this book were Sue Cymes and Patricia Barnes Mintz. The production supervisor was Lynn Basile. It was designed by Rosalie Carlson and set in Helvetica by University Graphics, Inc.

Printed and bound by Halliday Lithograph Corporation.
1234567890 HDHD 7654321098

Table of Contents

1. Introduction

The world's fastest-growing Gross National Product is that of Japan. Even after the shocks of the 1974 oil embargo, which tempered the pace of her industrial growth, Japan is continuing to advance the arts and sciences of the twentieth century with greater vigor, stamina and perseverance than any other single nation. The Japanese already extract ten million tons of coal each year from underwater mines,[1] they are considered "the greatest power in the world in industry based on microbiology,"[2] they caught Detroit napping with their development and implementation of the stratified-charge CVCC (compound vortex-controlled combustion) engine and the rotary engine,[3] and have been labeled by Herman Kahn as, "among the most forward-looking and future-oriented people in the world—if not the most so."[4] The reasons for this unprecedented growth and development are many, not the least of which is the determination to erase the humiliation suffered by the first total defeat in its 2,600-year history, which most of us are astonished to remember, occurred only one generation ago.

Paralleling this industrial progress is a desire to absorb, understand and appreciate all things Occidental. When I first visited Japan in 1968 I had the privilege of attending a concert of classical Western music performed by native Japanese with the precision and skill of an orchestra whose cultural heritage might well have been in Europe. At that time, the French bread and Danish pastry were abominable imitations of the genuine article, but by 1970 the diligent Japanese had sent a whole school of chefs and bakers around the globe to study the culinary arts. To my delight, by 1972 one could find in Tokyo, at Kinokuniya, Don Q or Andersen's, the equal of nearly any European or American dessert.

Japan's voracious appetite for Western culture includes an unbending determination to master modern architecture, and true to form, the designs, projects and buildings of the last two decades have begun setting a precedent for the rest of the world. The developments leading up to the present state of the art are marked by many innovative projects and various discarded dreams. Japan first captured the attention of the architectural world in 1960 with the simultaneous unveiling of Kenzo Tange's Plan for Tokyo and the publication of *Metabolism 1960* by five young designers who combined their diverse, futurist, urban concepts into one document. This so-called Metabolist Group consisted of four architects and one architectural journalist.

Changeability and flexibility were the key elements that the Metabolist Group seized upon and explored. *Metabolism,* as we know it, is the biological process by which life is maintained through the continuous cycle of producing and destroying protoplasm. To the Japanese architects who adopted the name, it meant creating a dynamic environment that could live and grow by discarding its outdated parts and regenerating newer, more viable elements. The idea, according to Noboru Kawazoe, was to develop a building system that "could cope with the problems of our rapidly changing society, and at the same time maintain stabilized human lives."[5]

The Metabolist manifesto was a collection of divergent viewpoints about the future of architecture and urban design. Along with Tange's Plan for Tokyo 1960, they focused attention on new Japanese solutions to the international problem of how to structure urban growth. So powerful were the images, and so compelling was the logic, that for more than a decade Western observers have been focusing on the Metabolists and their megastructures to the exclusion of the rest of Japan's recent architectural design. In this comprehensive survey we trace the development of the New Japanese Architecture from its early roots, in the 1920s, through that initial burst of energy in 1960, up to the present.

1.
Toshogu Shrine, Nikko, Seventeenth Century: Constructed to commemorate the life of Ieyasu Tokugawa (1542–1616), the entire complex represents the epitome of flamboyant forms and colorful, baroque ornamentation. (See color plate 171.)

Today Japanese architecture is far more than a collection of buildings based on foreign influences. It is in the mainstream of modern design, more aware of change and more sophisticated. Certain projects by architects like Kisho Kurokawa, Fumihiko Maki and Arata Isozaki have gone beyond derivation and imitation to achieve a sense of self-identity that is unique in its response to the program and to the site, generating an architecture of vitality and originality.

The time for us to perceive Japan as a reflection of Western thought is past. It is now time to appraise its architecture on its own terms, for its own merits and idiosyncracies, and for us to discuss not how it has been influenced, but rather how it will itself affect others.

Historical Perspective

On January 26, 1974, Emperor Hirohito and Empress Nagako celebrated their golden wedding anniversary commemorating 2,634 years of unbroken Imperial lineage. One reason for this impressive longevity is the resilience and adaptability of the Japanese. They have always been a people quick to recognize a more advanced foreign culture and eager to adapt those advances to their own civilization. Their culture has been inundated by foreign influence several times in its history. During the fifth and sixth centuries it borrowed technical skills, expertise, and philosophy from the Korean Silla and Han dynasties; during the eighth and ninth centuries it borrowed the alphabet, architecture, art and religion of T'ang dynasty China; and it borrowed again from the more advanced Chinese Sung dynasty in the thirteenth century. In each case, alien cultures were imported, studied, imitated and absorbed and finally given new life, being refined and molded into Japanese society. When Chinese culture was imported to Japan, the Japanese developed the saying, "Japanese spirit with Chinese learning." This attitude stressed borrowing external aspects of Chinese culture,

but altering them to fit into already-existing Japanese cultural patterns. For example, Chinese written characters were borrowed in meaning, but changed to fit Japanese sentence structure. In Chinese *benkyo* means "study." In Japanese the verb *suru,* meaning "to do," is attached to the Chinese characters creating *benkyo suru* (to do the act of studying), which eventually came to mean simply "to study." The same is true in present-day Japan where one will hear *taipu suru* (to type), or *standubai suru* (to stand by), in which Western concepts have been altered slightly and absorbed into everyday Japanese to the point where the common man often doesn't know what is foreign and what is native. This attitude proved to have a profound effect on the development of Japanese modern architecture as well. Western architectural design principles pioneered in Europe and America in the first half of the twentieth century have been borrowed and absorbed to the point where the average Japanese citizen is willing to accept them as part of his own national heritage. This has allowed the development of a very broad range of styles and an advanced technology that would seem revolutionary anywhere else in the world.

The Both/And Culture

An integral part of understanding the evolution of modern (Western) architecture in Japan requires a brief introduction to the culture and traditions of that country, and it is a nation steeped in tradition. Many of these traditions require rigid behavior within set cultural patterns, yet seem contradictory and puzzling to Americans and Europeans. In her classic book, aptly titled, *The Chrysanthemum and the Sword,* Ruth Benedict examines in detail the cultural attributes of a people who are "both aggressive and unaggressive, both militaristic and aesthetic, both insolent and polite, rigid and adaptable, submissive and resentful of being pushed around, loyal and treacherous, brave and timid, conservative and hospitable to new ways."[6] This ancient ability to accept two contradictory positions as the norm allows Japan to remain conservative yet be very avantegarde, and to continue in traditional ways yet adapt the very latest Western innovations.

This phenomenon of "Both/And" also occurs in architecture. According to Robert Venturi, Both/And architecture includes "elements that are both good and awkward, big and little, closed and open, continuous and articulated, round and square, structural and spatial. An architecture which includes varying levels of meaning breeds ambiguity and tension."[7]

A nation that can produce the elaborate and flamboyant Toshogu Shrine at Nikko and, during the same era, build the simple and serene Katsura Detached Palace is surely a Both/And culture. After examining modern Japanese buildings, we can add to Venturi's description, an architecture which includes elements that are both modern and traditional, technological and handcrafted, futurist and nostalgic, and natural and synthetic, as well as an architecture that is both hard and smooth, yet soft and flexible.

The culture of Both/And combines the past and present. The tradition of airing the *futon* (mattress or quilt) in the sun each day still occurs in modern-day Tokyo. The traditional attire is still worn in urban surroundings. The traditional *maiko* (apprentice *geisha*) still waits to greet the traveling Tokyo businessman arriving in Kyoto on the modern "bullet" train, (which follows the path of the historic Tohkaido road) just as her predecessors did several hundred years before. The traditional Sumo wrestling tournaments, once conducted as an "important religious rite,"[8] are still performed under the roof of a wooden Shinto shrine removed from the outdoors to sit below a modern reinforced-concrete stadium. The traditional banners announce the latest Kabuki performance or Sumo contest. Plastic signs and paper lanterns, clay tiles and cotton *koinobori* (carp), plexiglas plug-ins and paper *shoji* screens, all grace the complex and contradictory environment that is Japan today.

2.
Katsura Detached Palace, Kyoto, 1624: Built during the same era as the Toshogu Shrine, this elegant, simple pavilion reveals the Both/And nature of Japanese culture and design.

Six Hundred Years of Isolationism

After Japan absorbed the key elements of the thirteenth-century Chinese Sung and Yuan dynasties, she abruptly closed her doors to foreign influence and proceeded to develop a refined, carefully delineated and rigorously enforced internal structure and culture of her own. Sixteenth-century European sailing ships were turned away and the island country's unique 2,000-year-old culture became uniformly entrenched nationwide.

3

4

3.
The traditional *futon* and the laundry are aired in the Tokyo sunshine from the apartment above the family-owned mini-shop, as modern society and ancient ritual coexist in the dense urban fabric.

4.
The serene and delicate *maiko* wait to greet the Tokyo or Osaka businessmen in modern Kyoto Station, as their predecessors did hundreds of years before them.

It wasn't until Commodore Perry sent armed gunboats into Japanese waters in 1853 with an ultimatum to trade or else, that the by-now famous miracle of industrialization began. With the government's decision to open the country to Western influences, including the transition from a feudal, agrarian economy to an industrial economy, there also occurred a desire to build modern (Western-style) architecture.

The industrialization of Japan was a carefully orchestrated masterpiece conducted with deft precision by the central government. Building contracts were let primarily to government agencies which prevented the growth of independent architectural offices. Rigorous government regulations on building safety to guard against earthquake disaster fostered an emphasis on structural engineering rather than creative design, hindering the growth of modern architecture as an art form in Japan. In addition, the ancient saying, "Japanese spirit with Chinese learning," was transformed to, "Japanese spirit with Western learning." Noboru Kawazoe has explained that this attitude caused Japanese architects to use, "only the techniques and external forms of the industrial civilization of the West, without understanding its spiritual background. Consequently it was quite natural that they placed more stress on the engineering side in adopting Occidental custom."[9] This attitude is also evident in that the study of architecture was undertaken in the Department of Engineering at Tokyo University, the nation's single most prestigious institution. Given these dominating circumstances, Japanese architecture moved into the twentieth century as a stilted, dull imitation of European late-nineteenth-century Neoclassicism.

5

5.
A contemporary Tokyo couple takes a holiday stroll in traditional *kimono* attire. Although businessmen wear Western-style suits and ties during the working day, it is still customary to come home and relax in the timeless garments of Japan.

6.
A Japanese actress wears the hairdo of a *geisha*, complete with *kanzashi* ornaments. Genuine *geisha* still exist in Japan, but the art and talent of their ancestors is becoming increasingly rare.

7.
A Japanese actor wears the hairdo of a *samurai*, whose spirit and passion are manifest today in the devoted corporate businessman.

6

7

The fact that in 1923 the great earthquake destroyed nearly everything except buildings designed by Japanese structural engineers and the Imperial Hotel designed by Frank Lloyd Wright, gave an even stronger voice to the engineers. It also helped to launch the career of Wright's Czechoslovakian-born assistant, Antonin Raymond, who was actively engaged in the practice of architecture in Tokyo until his death on October 25, 1976, at the age of 88. According to Raymond, Wright's theory of earthquake design was "to make the walls thick and keep the building low," and the previously accepted theory of "floating foundations" is something of a fortunate fabrication.[10] Whether Raymond was right, or whether the foundations actually rested on caissons floating in the mud fields that Ieyasu reclaimed for his vassals, as Arthur Drexler suggested,[11] is for the engineers to resolve. In either case, the success of the Imperial Hotel and of other low buildings in withstanding the seismic tremors didn't go unnoticed by government officials who were quick to pass a post-earthquake height limitation of 100 feet (30m).

Aside from Raymond's elegant ferroconcrete International Style buildings and the limited work of a few others such as Sutemi Horiguchi and Tetsuro Yoshida, Japanese modern architecture dragged its feet. During the period just prior to the Second World War, militaristic chauvinism led government agencies to stipulate that public architecture must be of "a Japanese style founded in oriental taste."[12] This edict, combined with a ban on the use of steel for peaceful purposes issued in 1937, brought about an architecture combining imitation Western facades with Japanese roof tiles described by Kawazoe as having a "horrible anachronistic appearance."[13]

8

9

8.
The Kokugikan, built for modern *sumo* tournaments, holds 10,000 spectators; but the traditional Shinto Shrine has been suspended inside the stadium to allow the ancient religious ritual to be performed in its original setting.
9.
Two *sumo* wrestlers do battle today reminiscent of the legendary contests dating back to before the birth of Christ.
10.
Brightly colored *sumo* banners announce the day's contestants. The soft fabric contrasts with the concrete reality of urban Japan.

The Big Five Japanese Construction Companies

During the early years of the twentieth century, while Japanese engineers studied Western technology, the government fostered the study of European-style construction techniques among its craftsmen and artisans. Outside the government agencies where professional engineers controlled design, several so-called carpenter familes[14] were developing the expertise to build good reproductions of Occidental buildings. It should be noted that in preindustrial Japan, the ruling Tokugawa clan and their *daimyos* (rural administrative officials) employed these same carpenter families to design and build all government structures, many of which were intricately complex wooden buildings. In order to meet the challenge of their responsibilities, skilled carpenter families developed and became architect, engineer and contractor all in one. These families later played a key role in the development of Japan's modern architecture. They developed the ability to construct Western-style buildings while maintaining their triple role of designer-engineer-builder, and have since become

10

the backbone of Japanese construction technology. One such company is the Shimizu Construction Company which was founded by one of the oldest carpenter families. According to Antonin Raymond, in the twenties he personally taught Mr. Shimizu the art of building with reinforced concrete. However, in 1973 he admitted that, "Japanese technology has left me far behind."

The largest private construction company in Japan today also began as a family of craftsmen. It was founded in 1610 by a master craftsman named Takenaka Tobei Masataka, the official builder for Lord Oda. Three hundred years later, in 1909, descendants of the master craftsmen established Takenaka Komuten, or the Takenaka Construction Company. Today this interdisciplinary company employs nearly 9,000 people and has assets of one billion dollars. Apart from highly skilled architecture, engineering, and construction divisions, Takenaka has branches dealing with marketing management, construction management, and a very successful technical research laboratory which has developed some of the most advanced construction techniques in the world. It is remarkable that construction companies of this magnitude still manage to maintain a high level of design expertise. In the 1963 public competition for the National Theater, first prize was won by the design division of Takenaka Komuten, while entries from Shimizu Gumi (Shimizu Construction Co.) were awarded third prize, and first in the second-grade class. As recently as December 1973, Takenaka again won first prize in a national competition for high-rise, prefabricated housing units using a form of megastructure developed in their own research and development laboratories. The entry requirements

11, 12.
Traditional Japanese lanterns denote a local food store echoing the past, while plastic illuminated signs for McDonald's® adorn a contemporary Tokyo street.
13.
The annual ritual of hanging *koinobori* persists today. The colorful fish seem to swim upstream against the current and the ceramic tile and concrete of the city, symbolic of youth, perseverance and unbending optimism.

(as enumerated on page 40) for such a large-scale project are such that independent architects are all but ruled out of the competition. It is for these reasons that Japan's construction giants have had a strong influence on the development of a modern national architecture.

In addition to the Shimizu Construction Company and Takenaka Komuten, three other construction-company conglomerates have developed, comprising what has come to be called the Big Five. These include Kajima Corporation, Ohbayashi-Gumi, and Taisei Corporation. As a group,

they are reputed to control 40% of all construction in Japan. One key reason for this is that the companies have remained family owned and operated and have maintained the traditional master-disciple structure of feudal Japanese society, all but guaranteeing lifetime service from their employees.[15]

The Emergence of Modern Japanese Architecture

While the construction-company family enterprises built efficient, economically sound empires, stressing technological

13

expertise and pioneering the total design concept which included every phase of architecture from inception to completion, the growth of a philosophy or conceptual foundation for modern Japanese architecture was left to a few key individuals.

Antonin Raymond who had previously worked for Cass Gilbert on the Woolworth Building in New York, America's first noble high-rise office structure, arrived in Tokyo in 1919 with Frank Lloyd Wright to assist in the design and supervision of the Imperial Hotel. After the completion of the

16

hotel, Raymond opened his own studio in Azabu, Tokyo in 1921, which became the only source of Western architecture in Japan for many years.

During the 20s and 30s Raymond designed residential and institutional architecture combining his skill in the International Style with his fondness for natural materials which he inherited both from the Japanese and from Wright. He left Japan as World War II became an inevitability and lived in the United States. After the war he returned to Azabu to rebuild his home and his practice.

His *Reader's Digest Building* of 1950, designed with his partner Ladislav L. Rado and structural engineer Paul Weidlinger, and his American Embassy Apartments of 1951 incorporated cantilevered balconies, *brise-soleil*, (sun-screens) and modern construction technology with a clean, articulated, International Style aesthetic. *Architectural Forum*, in a nine-page, illustrated story commented that, "Traditional Japanese qualities of lightness and grace are expressed through modern concrete and steel."[16]

The Reader's Digest Building was razed in 1964 to make room for a high-rise office building. Les Rado remembers that, "It was considered by the Japanese profession as a postwar landmark building and there were protests in the press against taking it down. To no avail, of course."

Raymond's design for the Gunma Music Center, completed in 1961, represents the best in folded-plate, reinforced-concrete technology that had been achieved at that time. It is part of a long career in which Raymond stressed quality design and the advancement of the art of building.[17] Out

17

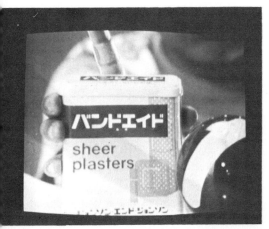

18

19

20

14, 15.
Contemporary Japanese magazines imitate their successful Western counterparts. The smiling soldier with the "peace" sign adorns the cover of a magazine whose name phonetically spells "PUNCH," after the English journal renowned for its dry wit and left-wing political leanings.
The magazine cover with the two little ladies in the center is a weekly entertainment and amusement journal, covering the latest in T.V., music, and the movies. Included in this issue is a "VIP Interview" with the Beach Boys. For sales purposes, the magazine's name phonetically spells "PLAYBOY®," although the contents bear little resemblance to the original.
16.
Japanese artists hand-paint the plastic food that sits in restaurant windows throughout the country. It is surreal in its accuracy and is produced for both the traditional cuisine and the latest imported delicacy.

17, 18.
Japanese T.V. commercials indicate that Western commercialism integrates easily into modern Japan.
19, 20.
Traditional kegs of *sake* (Japanese rice wine) are not far from the prefabricated plastic beer crates of a Both/ And culture.

of his studio came two of the giants of modern Japanese architecture, Kunio Maekawa and Junzo Yoshimura. Maekawa not only worked for Raymond for five years, but also spent several years in Paris in the office of Le Corbusier, where he worked on the Villa Savoye and the Swiss Pavilion. After Maekawa left Corbu's Atelier he was replaced by Junzo Sakakura who designed the Japanese Pavilion at the Paris World's Fair in 1937, winning the Grand Prix. Other serious students of Western architecture worked for Wright himself or studied with Gropius at the Bauhaus.

Bauhaus principles had a strong following in Japan during the 1930s. Not the least talented of these adherents to the Bauhaus were Tetsuro Yoshida and Sutemi Horiguchi. According to Arthur Drexler's in-depth review of Japanese Architecture published in 1955, "Horiguchi's Wakasa House, built in 1939, recalls the work of Walter Gropius in its asymmetric, cubic massing and structurally unarticulated stucco surfaces, but a long, narrow swimming pool at right angles to the house introduces a landscape-building relationship peculiarly Japanese."[18] Horiguchi continued to practice architecture in Ja-

21

22

21, 22.
Just as the *Deva* Kings, guardians of Buddhism who protected the temple gates, symbolized strength and power in the past, the modern-day Japanese "superfly" symbolizes the fearless strength that young boys in Japan dream about.

23, 24.
Gunma Music Center, Antonin Raymond and L. L. Rado, 1961: The concrete, folded-plate technology, and square-grid, glass-curtain wall were only two of the many advances made by Raymond in over fifty years of architectural practice in Japan.

25.
Harumi Apartments, Kunio Maekawa, 1958: Maekawa's experience working for both Antonin Raymond and Le Corbusier are evident in these apartment blocks reminiscent of Corbu's Unité d'Habitation in Marseilles.

pan as well as writing several fine books, including *Tradition of the Japanese Garden.*

Tetsuro Yoshida also followed modern German architectural concepts in his Tokyo Central Post Office of 1933. According to Noboru Kawazoe, "It was a forerunner of the perfected modern Japanese design of Kenzo Tange."[19]

It was at about this time that the German architect Bruno Taut came to Japan. "He applauded Tetsuro Yoshida in his writings as one of the world's master architects,

along with Frank Lloyd Wright, Walter Gropius, Mies van der Rohe, and Le Corbusier, and acclaimed the Tokyo Central Post Office as one of the masterpieces of modern times."[20] It was also Taut who called world attention to the Katsura Detached Palace and Ise Shrine as architectural wonders ranking with the Parthenon.

The most influential and devoted architect of this generation, however, was clearly Kunio Maekawa. In design competitions for public buildings calling for "Japanese style based on oriental taste," Maekawa submitted well-conceived, carefully orga-

nized entries designed in the International Style. Although his entries never won, his work was published, and in 1938 they attracted to his office a young graduate from Tokyo University's Department of Engineering by the name of Kenzo Tange.

Tange worked for Maekawa for four years, increasing his knowledge of Corbusier's ideas and of International Style principles. In 1941, with the outbreak of the Pacific War, Tange could find no work, so he rematriculated at Tokyo University to begin his lifelong study of urban design. During this phase of his development he stud-

23

24

25

ied the agora of ancient Greece, a meeting place, which was the basis of his "communication space principle" first formalized in the Plan for Tokyo 1960.

Tange developed the term "communication space" to fill a void in Japanese architectural vocabulary. In traditional Japan buildings were constructed along narrow paths without any public open space. Private gardens and inner courtyards were the only outdoor spaces in the urban fabric. The traditional European town square or *piazza* did not exist in Japan. Tange's

study of the Grecian agora revealed as he described it, "a meeting place where the citizens moved from the private realm to establish connections with society. As a meeting place—or what we today call a communications space—the agora presented a superb spatial image."

This image of large public open spaces, where people could meet and communicate with each other within the dense fabric of the city, was revolutionary in Japan, and Tange employed it as one of the basic principles of his urban design solutions.

In 1951, Tange attended the eighth CIAM *(Congrès Internationaux d'Architecture Moderne)* conference with his former mentor, Kunio Maekawa. The theme of the conference was "The Heart of the City," and Tange had the privilege of presenting his award-winning scheme for the reconstruction of Hiroshima. Looking back, Tange remembers that, "I was in my thirties then, and having the pleasure of meeting historical figures like Le Corbusier, Gropius, and Giedion was a thrill that I shall find difficult to forget."

26

26.
Wakasa House, Sutemi Horiguchi, 1939: An adherent of Walter Gropius and Bauhaus principles, Horiguchi's work evokes the massing and interpenetration of solid and void of the early International Style.
27.
The Family Tree of Modern Japanese Architecture attempts to explain, in graphic form, which of the major architects in each generation worked for whom.

Tange also visited Corbu's Unité d'Habitation which was under construction in Marseilles. He recalls that until that time, "no piece of architecture had moved me so much." The apparently well-received Hiroshima Plan combined with Tange's visit to Marseilles strengthened his convictions that major urban restructuring was, firstly, a viable notion and, secondly, seemed within the realm of reality by employing postwar Western technology.

During the fifties, Tange's continued contact with CIAM members, including Alison and Peter Smithson and Jacob Bakema, served to reinforce his concepts of urban infrastructure as patterns of communication and transportation. By 1957, Kenzo Tange & URTEC[21] were busily preparing for the Tokyo World Design Conference to be held in 1960. This was to be the postwar "coming-out" party for Japanese architects and urban designers. The focus of the international design community was clearly on Japan and this, undoubtedly, inspired both Tange and his team of designers to produce a most impressive Tokyo plan, as well as generating the birth of the Metabolist Group.

27

The Family Tree of Modern Japanese Architecture:

Developed by Michael Franklin Ross, AIA

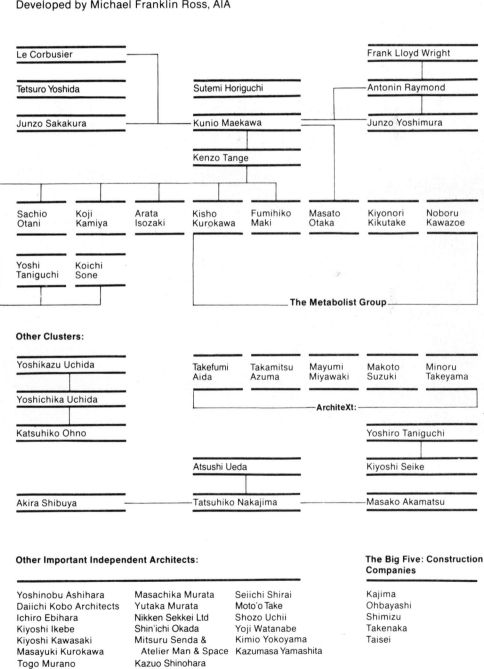

2.
Megastructuring: Urban Structures for the Expanding Metropolis

The year 1960 was a turning point in the history of Modern Japanese architecture. It was the year that Kenzo Tange and UR-TEC produced the radical Plan for Tokyo which spanned the Tokyo Bay in a series of megaclusters. It was the year that five young architects banded together to publish their avant-garde concepts in a manuscript which became their calling card. It was entitled, *Metabolism 1960.* The cumulative energies of a decade and a half of planning and conceptualizing that occurred after the end of the war in the Pacific were crystalized into two distinct, but not unrelated, urban design statements.

Tange's Plan for Tokyo proposed an alternative to the uncontrolled expanding metropolis. It called for an "information and communication" network capable of growth and change through the extension of parallel loops forming an extended spine that stretched from The Imperial Palace, in central Tokyo, across Tokyo Bay, to the suburbs of Chiba Prefecture. It was generated by the desire to structure the haphazard building and industrial growth which was rapidly engulfing the countryside. It sought the recovery of spatial order and the introduction of urban

communication spaces unknown in traditional Japanese cities. Tange explained that, "the traditional Japanese city has no plaza," only the street as communication spaces, and that, "we need more than just the street" as a gathering place for people. To satisfy this need, Tange introduced large urban spaces under ten-story-high sloping roofs, bridging off the central spine. These structures, based on his World Health Organization (WHO) scheme of 1960, later formed the genesis for the interior of the Tokyo Olympic Stadium, built in 1964.

In 1961, Tange and URTEC refined one section of the Plan for Tokyo and produced the Tsukiji Plan, which lifted the bridges up into the sky linking vertical communication spaces with each other across the urban void, weaving a three-dimensional lattice above the city. The bridges were supported by core shafts, 65 ft (20 m) square, planned at 245-ft (70–80 m) intervals. The shafts were service towers which contained vertical transportation, but had the structural capacity to support the bridges branching off of them as well as horizontal elements of a grid. These formed a Vierendeel truss-like space-frame giving rigidity to the cores.

The very idea of towers and bridges linking together the building blocks of the city into an over-all system was unsettling to some, but stimulating to everyone. It was a megastructure.

At about the same time that Tange was evolving this Plan for Tokyo, a group of young, concerned architects began meeting informally to exchange ideas on a similar subject: how to structure the rapid growth of Japan's cities. Stimulated by the World Design Conference being held in 1960, the five friends put together a collection of independent articles which they published under the name *Metabolism 1960.* It was not a unified manifesto, but its impact on the architectural profession was so great that the label "Metabolist" was pinned on each member for many years to come, even as their design concepts grew apart and the Metabolist theme became nearly invisible in the work of some members, while amplified in the designs of others.

The original five members were composed of four practicing architects and one architectural critic. The architects were Kisho (Noriaki) Kurokawa, Kiyonori Kikutake, Fumihiko Maki, and Masato Otaka. The critic and journalist was Noboru Kawazoe.

28.
Plan for Tokyo, Kenzo Tange & URTEC, 1960: This visionary scheme for expanding Tokyo across the bay in a linear series of interlocking loops was the initial generator of a decade of megastructuring proposals. Tange envisioned an urban spatial order that reflected the city's fluid movement system, creating a method of structuring that fostered flexibility and change.

29, 31.
Detail, Plan for Tokyo: The transportation network created a system of man-made links above the surface of the bay. Large sloping roofs enclosed major public plazas, which Tange labeled "communication spaces," branching off the main arterials.

30, 32.
National Gymnasium, Kenzo Tange & URTEC, 1964: For the 1964 Olympics Tange created a stunning public gathering place with large roofs sloping up to a linear skylight, based directly on the prototypical structures in his Plan for Tokyo.

In 1960, the Metabolists were a young, idealistic, and diverse group of individuals. Kurokawa was the youngest at 26, three years out of Kyoto University and a precocious designer in Tange's office. Kikutake was 32, and ten years out of Waseda University. He had established his own practice in 1953, three years out of school. Maki was also 32 years old, but far more traveled and sophisticated than any other member of the group. After graduating from Tange's studio at Tokyo University in 1952, Maki left Japan for America, where he received a Master of Architecture from Cranbrook Academy in 1953 and

a Master of Architecture from the Graduate School of Design at Harvard in 1954. Subsequently, he worked for Skidmore, Owings and Merrill in New York and for Sert, Jackson Associates in Cambridge. From 1956–1958 he was an assistant professor at Washington University's School of Architecture, and from 1958–1960 he traveled the Middle East, Europe and Asia on a grant from the Graham Foundation. He returned to Japan in 1960, where he served for a short time in Tange's office before opening his own consulting firm. Otaka, at 37, was the senior member of the group. He had graduated from Tange's post-graduate program at Tokyo University 11 years previously, and had been one of the key designers in Kunio Maekawa's office ever since. He eventually opened his own office the following year, in 1961.

In a sense, the publication of *Metabolism 1960* was an exploration into variations and alternative solutions to the megastructure principal set forth in Tange's Plan for Tokyo. Tange's megaform developed from the belief that certain elements of the urban environment change or require replacement at a much higher frequency than other elements. He explained that:

"Short-lived items are becoming more and more short-lived, and the cycle is shrinking at a corresponding rate. On the other hand, the accumulation of capital has made it possible to build in large scale operations. Reformations of natural topography: dams, harbors, and highways are of a size and scope that involve long cycles of time, and these are the man-made works that tend to divide the overall system of the age. The two tendencies— toward shorter cycles and toward longer cycles—are both necessary to modern life and to humanity itself." [22]

30

31

32

Based on this notion and confident that the architect could ascertain, through careful examination of the urban fabric, which aspects of the environment would require frequent change and which would be long lasting, Tange proceeded to develop his megastructuring principles. The Plan for Tokyo was designed around the idea that transportation technology would change at a far slower rate than residential building technology. The infrastructure or skeleton is made up of highways, bridges, and communication channels as well as the physical structural frame which can accept a variety of interchangeable plug-in residential and office units. Tange reiterated that:

"By incorporating elements of space, speed and drastic change in the physical environment, we created a method of structuring having elasticity and changeability."[23]

Adaptability to change was the basic ingredient common to all Metabolist projects. Different members of the group developed the idea in different ways. Maki and Otaka coauthored an article which explored the concept of Group Form, which they said was, "an effort to create a new total image in order to express the vitality of our society, at the same time embracing individuality and retaining the identity of individual elements."[24] Group Form was distinct from megaform in that it was less rigid. It sought the vernacular aesthetic system of the village, the hill-town or the clustering of the town bazaar. Eventually the term Metabolism was developed into the concept of Metamorphosis, which was concerned with changes in the physical form and structure of cities that could respond to the needs of a dynamic society. From each member of the group, variations on the megaform theme, originally set forth in Tange's Plan for Tokyo, began to emerge.

33

33, 34.
Tsukiji Plan, Kenzo Tange & URTEC, 1961: This
detailed development of one segment of the Plan for
Tokyo introduced vertical core shafts and major bridge
elements linking the towers.

34

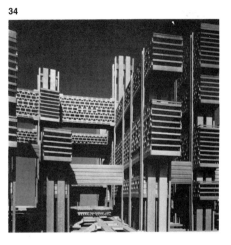

35, 36, 38.
City in the Sky, Arata Isozaki, 1962: These seminal studies apparently had a profound influence on the Tange design staff, of which Isozaki had been a prominent member.

37.
Yamanashi Communications Center, Kenzo Tange & URTEC, 1966: The first realization of the megastructure concept complete with vertical core shafts and horizontal floors "bridging" between them. (See color plates 173–175.)

39.
Detail, Yamanashi Communications Center: The core shafts at Yamanashi are a direct descendant of Isozaki's City in the Sky sketches.

40.
Shizuoka Press and Broadcasting Office, Kenzo Tange & URTEC, 1967: On a difficult triangular site, Tange created a single core shaft with cantilevered offices, as another experimental piece in his visionary megastructural puzzle.

35

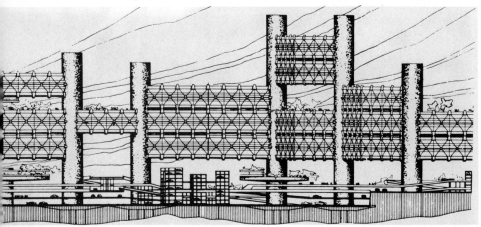

36

37

In 1962, a young architect working in Tange's office by the name of Arata Isozaki, published a series of sketches he called the "City in the Sky." Although friendly with members of the Metabolist Group, Isozaki was not a member and developed his concepts and drawings independently. His designs exhibited an apparent involvement with Tange's earlier work, but brought a certain fresh, visionary quality that was unmistakably his own.

The City in the Sky called for a city infrastructure employing cylindrical joint cores 650 ft (200 m) high that acted as the structural and mechanical trunks to serve the horizontal arms branching off of them. These, in turn, supported plug-in residential units. It was a highly technological, geometrical abstraction of interlocking trees. A prophetic design, the City in the Sky concept was realized four years later, in 1966, on a smaller scale, by Kenzo Tange & URTEC, at the Yamanashi Communication Center, and again in 1967 in the Shizuoka Press and Broadcasting Office. Looking back on Isozaki's contribution in the development of the megastructure, Tange admits with the humility of a great man that, "we influenced each other."

At about the same time that Isozaki was producing the City in the Sky, Kurokawa designed his Helix City, and Kikutake developed a series of proposals for cylindrical floating cities, beginning with rough sketches in 1958, which evolved into his Ocean City of 1961, and later the Marina City of 1963.[25] Every scheme was based on long-term service towers which, in one way or another, supported and served

38

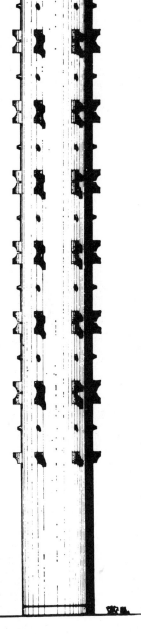

39

40

short-term living spaces. Kurokawa's Helix City, twisting its way up into space, linked the towers together with a horizontal infrastructure in a fashion that could bridge across land or sea. Kikutake's Ocean City, 1961, envisioned cylindrical towers set on circular pads floating on the water. The Marina City, 1963, proposed the cylindrical towers growing directly out of the ocean. Rather than bridges linking the towers together, Kikutake proposed little round minicapsules that could be plugged into the towers or replaced as needed. It was the first scheme that pro-

posed independent, unconnected capsule towers, about one year before Archigram's[26] Warren Chalk refined the idea into his Capsule Homes Tower, and nearly ten years before the concept was finally realized in several locations in Japan.

Maki and Otaka never produced megastructural schemes for entire cities which focused on industrial technology. They concentrated instead on generic Group Form and space studies, such as their Shinjuku Redevelopment Project. This was followed, in 1965, by Maki's Golgi

Structures which were based on the biological model of the Golgi body, named for Camillo Golgi, a nineteenth-century Italian physiologist noted for his basic research in neurology. In 1883 his studies of the central nervous system revealed multipolar cells which had the ability to establish connections with other nerve cells. This research eventually led another scientist to the discovery of the neuron, which constitutes the structural and functional unit of nerve tissue.

Like his fellow Metabolists, Maki found biological models most appropriate to de-

41

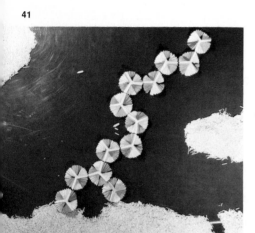

42

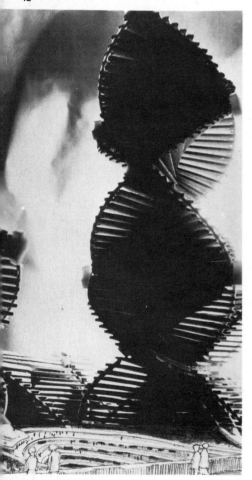

43

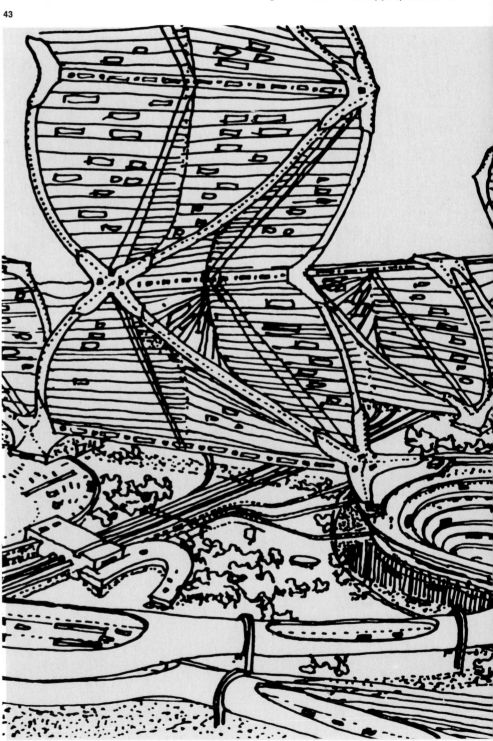

scribe the theories he espoused; but there was a clear distinction. The other members of the group talked about "metamorphosis," and focused on changes in the physical form utilizing industrial technology to realize their visions. Maki was less concerned with high technology and more concerned with space and the relationship of solid to void. He considered how people might react to an urban environment and, using Golgi's idea, considered how multipolar nerve centers in the city have the ability to establish connections with other centers. From these observations he developed his Golgi Struc-

41–43.
Helix City, Kisho (Noriaki) Kurokawa, 1961: Kurokawa's first independent megastructure after working for Tange on the Plan for Tokyo. His Helix City also stretched across the water and connected vertical shafts with a horizontal infrastructure of bridge elements.

44.
Ocean City, Kiyonori Kikutake, 1961: This proposal was a refinement of Metabolist sketches Kikutake had made as early as 1958. The scheme called for plug-in capsules set into freestanding core shafts sitting on floating man-made pads. (See figures 342–349.)

44

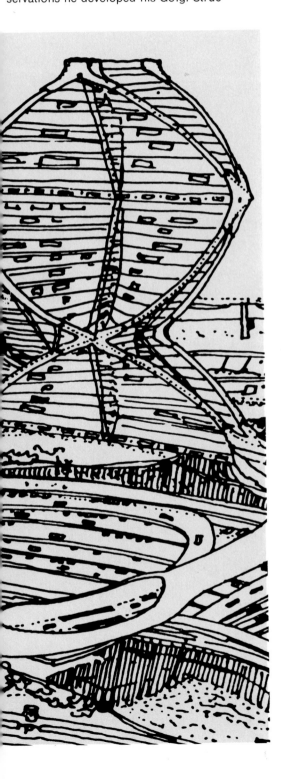

tures which he explains, "show how the interior space of a building can be conceived as a direct function of a certain order of preconceived exterior spaces, which first serve as the generators of the interior spaces, and become eventually the interior space themselves."

In the models that Maki created, he began by designing the voids in the city structure. Most people perceive the urban environment as masses of buildings (solids), while the streets, courtyards, parks and alleys (voids) occur as leftover space. Maki began instead by designing a hier-

archy of urban spaces. This preconceived exterior void took the form of cylinders and cones in his highly abstract models. As the built environment developed, the solids began to fill in the areas around these voids, so that the exterior spaces evolved into large urban rooms with the qualities of interior public spaces. The various elements of the Golgi Structures include: a communication space containing vertical transit, energy distribution and mechanical systems; a light membrane defined by a skin of light-absorbing cells; and specific spaces generated by the voids.

Realization of the First Megastructure

The following year, 1966, was a triumph for Kenzo Tange & URTEC. The dream of building a megastructural system of interlocking shafts, bridges, and communications spaces, which had been promulgated by Tange and his disciples, was achieved for the first time at the Yamanashi Communications Center. High in the mountains of Kofu, Yamanashi Prefecture, Tange created a three-dimensional network composed of 16 concrete shafts with prefabricated "teeth" to receive the

45

46

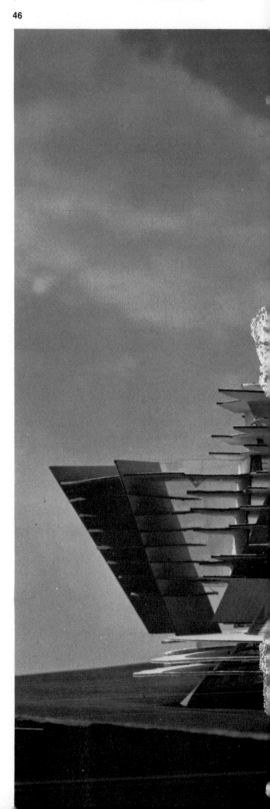

45, 46.
Golgi Structures, Fumihiko Maki, 1965: Maki's entrant in the megastructure game was more dense and sophisticated than previous schemes, attempting to evolve the form of the city from preconceived urban spaces.

bridges linking the towers together. The shafts serve the bridged spaces by housing elevators, ducts, stairs, and toilets. The voids left between the shafts imply the potential for future growth and flexibility. In 1974, Tange & URTEC were retained to design an extension to the building, and, as proof of their basic thesis, employed the same design elements and construction techniques used in the original facility.

In retrospect, the finished building, which was developed out of Tange's earlier plans for restructuring whole portions of urban centers, rises above the traditional tile roofs like something out of another age. An astounding achievement in the development of the megastructuring concept, the concrete shafts tower over the nineteenth-century landscape wishing they were part of an over-all urban network.

In the latter part of 1966, Tange was invited by the editors of *Shinkenchiku* (*The Japan Architect*) to judge a residential design competition whose central theme was "the nature of urban dwellings and their connecting systems." From among the 328 entries, Tange selected a sophisticated megastructure by Akira Shibuya as the winner. It was a remarkable solution which seemed to integrate into one super-megastructure all of the visionary notions of Tange, Isozaki, the Metabolists, and the recently published ideas of Archigram. Unquestionably influenced by Tange's Tsukiji Plan, it nonetheless managed to improve upon it in several important ways. There were the basic erector set components of shafts and bridges, but there was also an awareness of future urban transportation systems and a flexibility in the use of prefabricated capsules suspended

from the bridges. There was the introduction of man-made parks and community gathering places above the noise and traffic of the city streets. Each unit was a duplex, offering a private terrace and garden in the tradition of Japanese residential architecture. Tange's comments on the solution noted that, "Though a number of similar proposals have already come forth, in this case the designer has added some new ideas, has thoroughly worked out his theoretical assembly, and has given the whole a certain plastic-form appeal that makes the entry superior."[27]

Shibuya's winning entry was followed by lesser schemes which examined the various potentials of the megastructure *ad nauseam*.

As the sixties began to draw to a close, it became painfully apparent that all the expectations raised by Tange and the Metabolist Group in architectural circles throughout the world were not about to become reality. At the end of the decade, only one physical example had been completed. The urban centers of Japan, though planned better than they had been in the past, remained largely a haphazard blanket of one-, two-, and three-story walk-ups, crammed into the available space. The government legislation, the land acquisition, the financing, and the public support necessary to create a new urban prototype was not available. Undaunted, individual members of the movement continued to build their architectural practices, always mindful that each separate building was part of a larger whole, and always seeking the opportunity to express that relationship when the circumstances allowed.

47

48

47–49.
Urban Megastructure, Akira Shibuya, 1966: The culmination and distillation of ideas from Metabolism to Archigram. In this competition-winning scheme Shibuya integrates core shafts, bridges and capsules with the latest in high-technology transportation.
50–52.
Plans, Urban Megastructure: Plastic modules suspended from the concrete bridges are designed to be adapted or discarded and replaced.

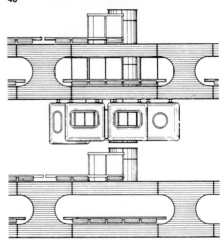

Expo '70, in Osaka, gave many architects the opportunity to vent their frustrations, creating one of the most stimulating displays of industrial technology in architecture ever assembled in one location. The over-all structure of the site was designed by Kenzo Tange & URTEC, while many individual pavilions were contributed by members of the Metabolist Group. Kikutake designed the tower, complete with clusters of geodesic domes, the insides of which he filled with murals of his visionary Marina City proposing more towers and more capsule clusters. Kisho Kurokawa designed several pavilions, including the Celestial Theme Pavilion and the Takara Beautilion. Both designs proclaimed the virtues of the new technology employing space frames, capsule clusters, and sophisticated electronic equipment, to awaken the masses to the potential of Metabolist architecture. And finally, Arata Isozaki filled the Festival Plaza with joy and wonder by devising a system of computer-operated components which programmed the movements of the grandstand, the stage, the overhead lights, and the machinations of his walking, talking, light-up mechanical man.

49

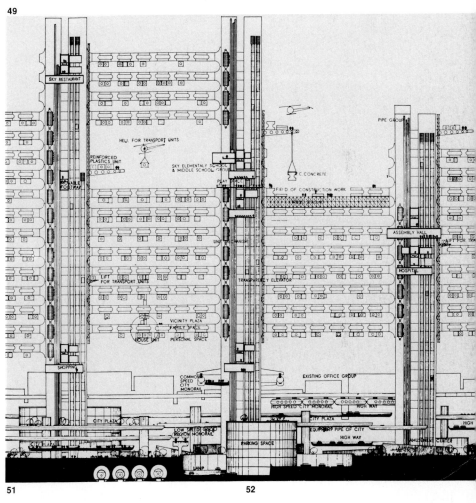

50

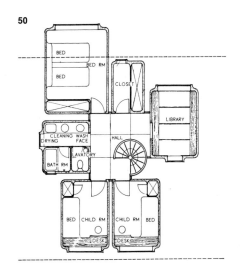

51 **52**

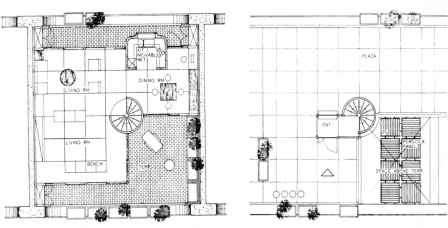

53.
Celestial Theme Pavilion, Kisho Kurokawa, 1970:
Designed for Expo '70 and containing an ''Information
Tree'' of television sets, this visionary cluster of
capsules proposed a flexible, expandable, plug-in
residence.
54.
Takara Beautilion, Kisho Kurokawa, 1970: Also
designed for Expo '70. This futuristic pavilion
exaggerated the image of technology and the concept
of flexibility by creating an interlocking space frame
with a multiple of stainless-steel capsules.
55.
Sapporo Labor Welfare Center, Kisho Kurokawa, 1971:
An early Kurokawa attempt at prefabricated concrete
box units, which was later refined to a more lightweight, flexible enclosure.
56.
Nakagin Capsule Building, Kisho Kurokawa, 1972: By
using the shipping container as a model, Kurokawa
developed this prototypical high-rise megastructure of
concrete towers and welded steel capsules. (See
figures 128–139.)

Kisho Kurokawa: A Capsule Summary

It was Kurokawa, however, who championed the use of capsules and industrialized technology in the early seventies. He developed prototypical living modules that could be fabricated at a price competitive with existing housing methods. He worked with the manufacturers of shipping containers to uncover the most economical methods for manufacturing, transporting, and assembling box-like units into environments for people. At first he tried precast concrete units at the Sapporo Labor Welfare Center, but they proved too cumbersome. Then he tried a welded steel frame enclosed in an insulated jacket which proved more flexible and economical. In late 1972 he unveiled his Nakagin Capsule Building as a prototypical part of a larger megastructural whole. It was reminiscent of earlier schemes in that it was composed of towers connected at various levels by pedestrian bridges. The towers acted as service cores in a similar manner to those at Yamanashi, housing elevators, mechanical equipment, and stairs. The Nakagin Capsule Building attempted to reassert the viability of large-scale urban structuring methods and proved that such structures could be built and marketed in dense downtown Tokyo, where land costs rival those of any city in the world.

Kurokawa has also applied his concept of multistructure to the design of high-rise office buildings. His more recent studies for the Osaka Sony® Tower as an "information tree," completed in 1976, exemplify his indefatigable devotion to testing a given technology against various situations. Both in the early study model and the completed building, Kurokawa em-

55

56

ploys prefabricated capsules to house the mechanical functions. He explains today, as he did in 1960, that his paramount concern is flexibility and ease of interchangeability of parts. This is the rationale for attaching the relatively short-term mechanical elements on the exterior. This is, however, in direct opposition to earlier designs in which the mechanical equipment found itself locked in vertical core-shafts. Undoubtedly his experience with previous capsule towers and the rapid changes in mechanical technology have caused Kurokawa to shift the capsules to the easily accessible outer periphery.

Government Housing Employs Metabolist Principles

At the same time that Kurokawa was convincing the private sector that megastructuring techniques could turn a profit, the Government had been conducting its own investigation into the housing industry. Under the sponsorship of the Ministry of Construction, design competitions were held to stimulate the development of more advanced building techniques and to achieve the most economical solution to housing problems. In order to foster serious research into building technology and to test the viability of the entries, the competition winners were awarded sizeable building contracts by the Japan Housing Corporation. One of the most successful of these competitions was the Pilot House Project, undertaken in 1970. It called for the design of both single-family and multiple dwelling systems to be erected in the same community, forming the residential sector of a new town. Although the solutions lacked some of the aesthetic-of-the-future appeal of the Metabolists, they did pioneer new building techniques, brought about the production of new materials meeting more rigorous specifications, and they proved to the satisfaction of even their staunchest opponents that industrialized building technology could outperform traditional methods and materials in almost every respect. Some of the best-conceived solutions included the single-family row houses by Ohbayashi-Gumi, and the multiple dwellings of Tokyu Prefab and Mitsui Zosen.

The success of the Pilot House Project encouraged the Japanese government to sponsor competitions that would encompass more complex and sizeable urban

58

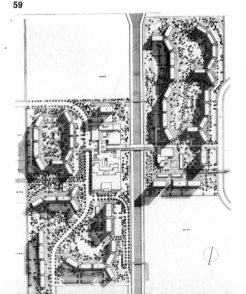

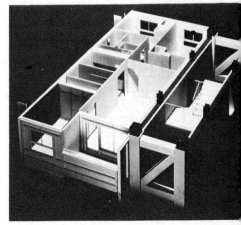

57.
Osaka Sony® Tower, Kisho Kurokawa, 1976: A full-scale realization of the "information tree" concept that first appeared in Kurokawa's Celestial Theme Pavilion. The tower combines high-tech, stainless-steel capsules with a mixture of glass and metal skin to symbolize the technologically advanced products of the Sony® Company.
58–60.
Ashiyahama New Community, Takenaka Construction Company, 1977: The winner of a national competition held in 1973, this scheme combines futuristic Metabolist concepts with pragmatic construction technology.

community development. In 1973, this brought about the Ashiyahama High-Rise Housing competition for reclaimed land outside of Osaka, jointly sponsored by the Japan Housing Corporation and the Japan Architectural Center. The objective of the competition was to develop an experimental city of 3,400 low-cost dwelling units by means of industrialized technology. The detailed submission requirements called for not only architectural design drawings, but definitive descriptions of the production systems, construction systems, construction materials transportation, soil engineering, apartment build-

ing administration and maintenance, emergency planning, and construction costs. The chief juror of the competition was Professor Yoshichika Uchida of Tokyo University, the nation's authority on industrialized building systems.

Of the more than twenty-five sets of entries, first prize was awarded to a joint venture team called ASTM (Ashiyahama Shin'nittetsu Takenaka Matsushita). It was an inventive team directed by the Takenaka Komuten design and construction firm, which collaborated with the Nippon Steel Corporation (Shin'nittetsu) to de-

velop the structure, and with Matsushita Kosan Co., a division of Matsushita Electric Works, Ltd. (Panasonic®), to plan the real-estate development. The site planning advisor interestingly enough was one of the original Metabolists, Fumihiko Maki.

By integrating the multidisciplined expertise of the team members, ASTM achieved an intelligent site plan, a good mixture of medium- and high-rise elements, and an extremely interesting building system, all at a marketable price. The 14- to 29-story apartment units have been constructed

61

62

63

64

using a megastructural steel-truss framework into which more than 125 different prefabricated units are inserted. At first glance, the design seems almost ordinary compared to the futurist images put forth by the Metabolists a decade before; however, closer inspection reveals an infrastructure of large vertical shafts and bridges linking together the urban community at a series of horizontal levels. This megaframework employs deep trusses which give structural rigidity to the frame, while simultaneously opening every fifth floor of the structure to an outdoor communal green space. What ASTM has done

is to take the scale of the five-story row house and stack them in space. With the traditional Japanese concept of a man's home being on land foremost in their minds, the designers sought to create what they called *jinko tochi,* meaning "man-made land." These "midair parks" if you will, offer communal play spaces free from traffic, and provide economical access to the units, which are never more than two stories from a park. The megaframework itself also eliminates large structural members from the floor plans of the housing units, increasing the net usable floor area, and making possible a flexi-

ble wall system which can be continuously changed to fit the needs of growing families and transient tenants.

Units are all designed on a module of 3 ft (0.9 m) and vary in size from 560 sq ft (52 m²) to 900 sq ft (84 m²). The average construction cost per unit would have been about $15,000 in 1977. Factory-made utility cores for kitchen and bathrooms, complete with ducts, piping, and wiring, are inserted by crane on site. Wall and floor panels are made of lightweight, precast concrete. Floor slabs are 9 in (230 mm) thick, with styrofoam-filled cores to re-

65

66

61–64.
Ashiyahama New Community: Takenaka's Technical Research Laboratory developed an economical system of steel towers and bridges that accept a wide variety of prefabricated plug-in housing units.
65, 66.
Tochigi Prefectural Conference Hall, Masato Otaka, 1970: One of the best of the precast concrete, interlocking structures, evoking Japan's traditional wood, post-and-beam aesthetic. (See color plate 176.)

duce weight and transportation costs.

The site itself is 50 acres (203,000 m²), of which only 64% was allowed to be built upon. The land is divided by the Miya River separating the complex into two sections. All vehicular-access and parking areas are restricted to the periphery, reducing noise and exhaust pollution while creating a spine of community clusters, each with its own sense of identity and ground-level park.

Masato Otaka: Hiroshima Housing

At the same time that the Japan Housing Corporation was sponsoring competitions to foster progressive and economical solutions to the development of urban communities, various members of the Metabolists and their contemporaries were evolving solutions of their own. This group included Masato Otaka, Sachio Otani and Kiyonori Kikutake. Otaka had coauthored the article on Group Form with Maki in 1960. He had become a disciple of, and strong believer in, the principles of Kunio Maekawa, who had worked for Le Corbusier and who had been Tange's employer and mentor at one time.

With land at a premium, in 1963 Otaka generated his plan for the Sakaide Urban Platform using air rights over transportation corridors for urban housing. He also became interested in employing traditional Japanese interlocking-wood construction techniques in his contemporary structures. This idea created a common bond among architects in postwar Japan. Aware of the great social heritage of their nation, architects sought to preserve a

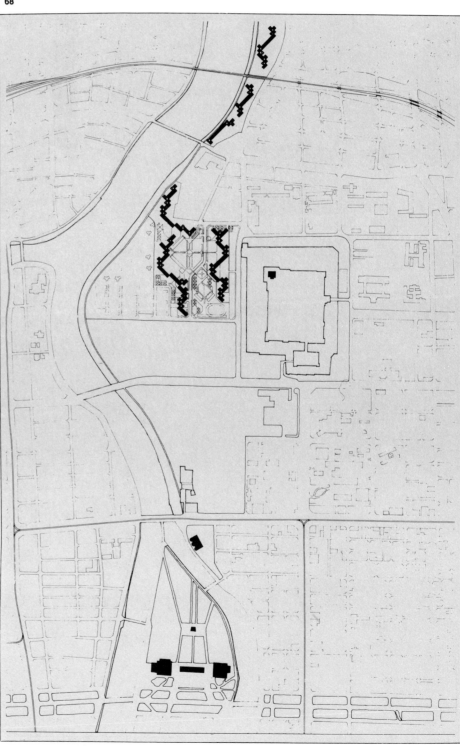

1. Peace Boulevard
2. Main Hall
3. Exhibition Hall
4. Auditorium
5. Peace Plaza
6. Peace Arch
7. Memorial Arbor
8. Dome
9. Children's Center
10. Library
11. Museum
12. Recreation Park
13. Football Field
14. Gymnasium
15. Tennis Courts
16. Wrestling Arena
17. Track Stadium
18. Swimming Pool
19. Boat House
20. Amphitheater
21. Science Museum
22. Art Museum
23. Library

sense of culture while at the same time employing the latest methodologies for rebuilding their urban communities. The logical solution was to use precast, reinforced concrete recalling the post-and-beam frameworks they had been surrounded by in their youth. One of the purest examples of this technique can be seen in Otaka's Tochigi Prefectural Council Building, designed in 1967 and completed in 1970. Employing a system of precast horizontal and vertical members, Otaka achieved a variety of spaces commensurate with the building program and in harmony with the wooden structural

systems prevalent in the immediate environment.

In 1968 Otaka was commissioned to develop an urban renewal plan for housing the squatters of Motomachi and Chojuen; two slum areas that had grown by necessity out of the ashes of Hiroshima.

The program called for 4,500 units to house a population of 15,000 people. It was an opportunity to apply the research he had been conducting with Maki on urban structuring and Group Form. A challenging assignment, the site was the same

one that Tange had designed in 1950 to be an extension of his award-winning Hiroshima Peace Park. Otaka was confronted with the problem of economically housing 15,000 inhabitants while trying to preserve the notion of a river-front park, envisioned by Tange, but never realized. The long, narrow site did not lend itself to the core shafts and bridges being investigated by his colleagues. Instead, Otaka developed a system of stepped blocks which he says, "are suggestive of the form of a folding screen." The ingenious solution affords every unit a view of the Ota River or of the historical Hiroshima Castle, and achieves

69

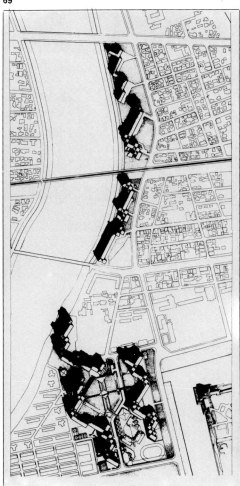

70

67.
Master Plan for Hiroshima Peace Park, Kenzo Tange & URTEC, 1950: The competition-winning scheme called for a major green spine along the river linking the ancient castle with the new Peace Plaza and Exhibition Hall.

68–70.
Hiroshima Housing, Masato Otaka, 1973: By stepping the housing units in plan and section, Otaka created a transition from low to high density while maintaining the maximum amount of public open space, in keeping with Tange's original concept of a linear park.

a green spine reminiscent of Tange's original design.

The entire complex manages to achieve a sensitive hierarchy of scales beginning with eight stories near the castle and stepping up to 20 stories along the river. Each stair tower acts as a fulcrum with the apartment blocks stepped around it. At this location Otaka has created a large communal space at each elevator lobby. By employing a skip-floor system he also achieves a more efficient net-to-gross floor ratio.

71

72

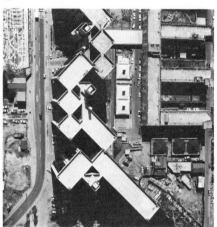

73

71–73.
Hiroshima Housing: Partially completed, the stepped housing blocks linked by vertical circulation towers already express Otaka's intent of giving every unit a major view of the river or the ancient Hiroshima Castle and surrounding moat.
74, 75.
Typical Floor, Hiroshima Housing: The single-loaded corridor and skip-floor section maximizes natural ventilation and private open space.
76.
Axonometric, Hiroshima Housing: Evoking the interlocking Metabolist proposals of the 60s, this elegantly detailed solution creates public parks on grade and on all roof areas.

The entire roof of every apartment is given over to public open space creating a continuous stepping park of interlocking platforms in which one can take extended strolls with constantly changing views and without every encountering a vehicular intersection. Considerable care has been taken to bring the greatest amount of green space to this high-density housing project (546 people per acre; 1,350 people per hectare). By applying the same concept developed for the Sakaide Urban Platform, Otaka has designed the main shopping center to be half a level down with a large central green space as its roof. This affords shoppers continuous cover during inclement weather and, of course, vastly expands the amount of usable public open space. According to governmental regulation, all housing projects must have community facilities. Motomachi and Chojuen, like the ASTM Ashiyahama Project, include schools, meeting and conference facilities, a rest home for the elderly, fire and police departments, shops, a hospital, public baths, and administrative offices.

Sachio Otani: Kawaramachi New Community

The evolution of the career of Sachio Otani in many ways parallels that of Masato Otaka. Otaka received his Bachelor of Architecture degree from Tokyo University in 1947, did graduate work until 1949, then apprenticed himself to Kunio Maekawa for 12 years, from 1949 to 1961, gradually working his way up to be the master's chief designer. Otani received his Bachelor of Architecture degree from the same university one year earlier, in 1946. He en-

74

75

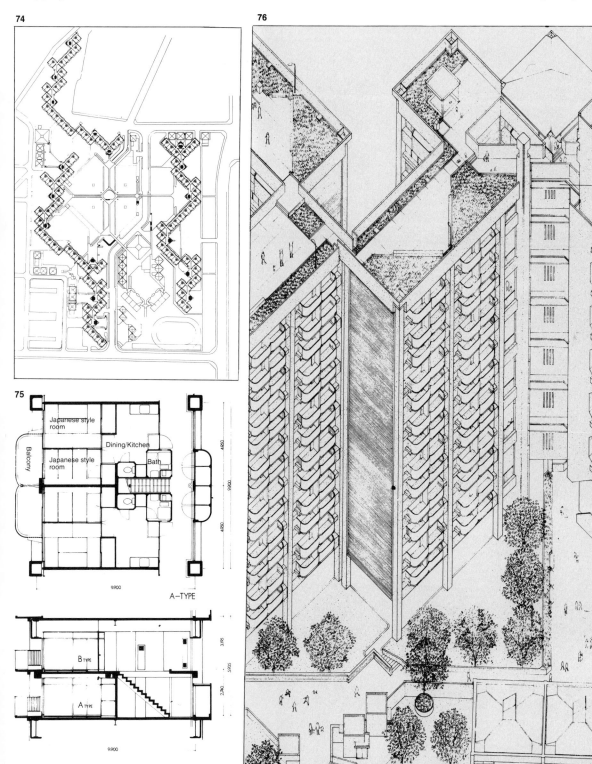

Japanese style room

Dining/Kitchen

Balcony

Japanese style room

Bath

4860

9900

4860

9900

A–TYPE

3195

5905

2240

B TYPE

A TYPE

9900

76

rolled in the post-graduate program the following year, while simultaneously beginning his 14-year employ in the office of Kenzo Tange. Otani, like Otaka, grew up in a Japan where job mobility is frowned upon and where the master-disciple relationship is the foundation of the social structure. He too served his master faithfully until he became Tange's chief designer and assistant at Tokyo University. Today, Otani has inherited Tange's studio in the Department of Urban Engineering.

In the early sixties, Otani began his independent practice, focusing on some of the

same problems as the Metabolist Group; urban structuring and how to relate new technology to traditional cultural values. He developed a high-density, low-rise housing system for the Kojimachi District and began investigating methods for using reinforced-concrete technology. He was catapulted into the public eye in 1963, when awarded first prize in the design competition for the Kyoto International Conference Hall.

The building is the epitome of interlocking precast-concrete technology, aesthetically founded on traditional wooden post-

and-beam Japanese architecture. The section of the building, according to Otani, was developed in response to the angle of the sun. This may well be, but the over-all visual system, the overlapping sloping planes interconnected with exposed structural members, is certainly indebted to the seventh-century Shinto Shrines of Ise and Izumo for its inspiration.

Set on Takaragaike Pond, the building rests like a massive concrete ship in dry dock. The bold geometry, the interpenetration of solid and void, and the dexter-

77, 78.
Kyoto International Conference Hall, Sachio Otani, 1966: A massive display of precast concrete technical virtuosity that reminds us of the ancient Japanese shrines of Ise and Izumo, with its slanting, interlocking structural members. (See color plate 177.)
79.
Ise Shrine: First constructed during the period of 250 to 500 A.D. By the end of the seventh century, the custom of rebuilding the entire shrine every twenty years was established.
80–84.
Kawaramachi New Community, Sachio Otani, 1973: Based on the Master Plan of 1969, this high-density community employs inverted Y-shaped towers to create stepped housing units, each with a private outdoor space.

78

79

ous use of precast components influenced an entire generation of Japanese designers. To many it was a successful fusion of contemporary technology with traditional aesthetics.

As a member of Tange's office and research laboratory at Tokyo University for many years, Otani developed a rich understanding of the art and science of urban design. Himself a fine architect, Otani was also deeply concerned over the schism in Japan between the new technology and the past value of man's relation to nature. The postwar fanatic devotion to rebuilding

and industrialization had created a megalopolis from Tokyo to Osaka. The rice paddies which formerly filled the countryside were being replaced with steel refineries, manufacturing plants, and flimsy, densely packed dwelling units. One of the least desirable environments for human habitation in all of Japan was the industrial section between Tokyo and Yokohama, called Kawasaki. In 1969, one year after Otaka began work on redeveloping Hiroshima, Otani was invited to prepare a comprehensive housing and new-community plan for a 33.6-acre (13.6 ha) site in Kawasaki, called Kawaramachi. The prob-

lems facing Otani were similar to those faced by Otaka. The program called for 3,591 dwelling units at a density greater than 400 people per acre (1,000 people per hectare). Both men were charged with the responsibility of creating new homes for nearly 15,000 people which would vary in size from 390 sq ft (36 m²) to 475 sq ft (44 m²). Small quarters were not uncommon in Japan, but in structures housing upwards of one thousand people, the need for carefully planned communal space was of paramount importance.

Otani developed an inverted Y-shaped

80
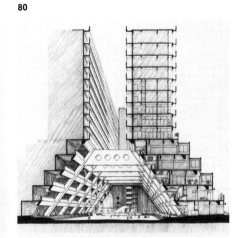

81
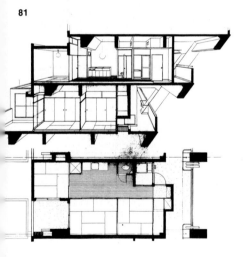

82
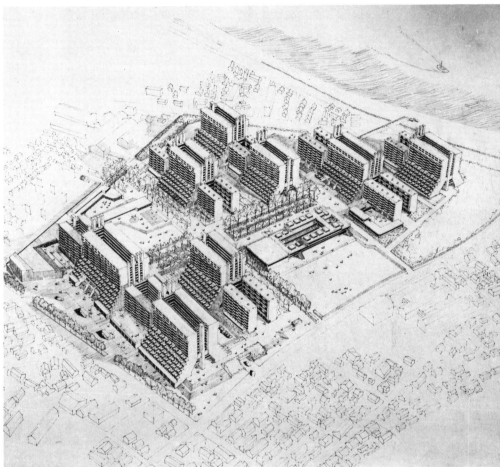

83

84

section reminiscent of Tange's gently curving walls rising to an open skylight in his Plan for Tokyo of 1960. This produced a communal play area within earshot of mama, while concurrently increasing the amount of sunlight reaching the lower units, which in most housing projects find themselves primarily in the shadow of the neighboring building. By orienting all the apartment blocks along a north-south axis, and by stepping the lower units like an open chest of drawers, Otani managed to achieve a minimum of three hours of southern sun exposure for every dwelling unit, even during the winter sun's low azi-muth angle. In addition, the building's shape allowed Otani to bring the 15-story structures closer together, gaining the required density and freeing other areas for needed outdoor open space.

In the design of low-income urban housing, when confronted by high densities and low budgets, it is often difficult to achieve an environment with a clear hierarchy of public, semipublic, and private open space; but Otani and his team of designers, including Messrs. Inaoka, Okabe, and Imai, managed to do it. Within the confines of a tightly woven urban fab-

85

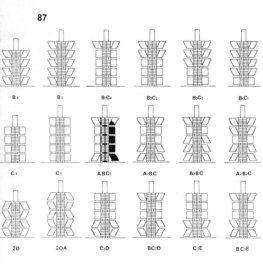

86

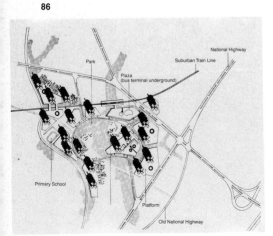

87

88

ric, and on a meager budget of $18.50 per sq ft, they fashioned a series of mini-hill-towns with outdoor patios for private enjoyment of the sunshine. The interior city-room suffers from the lack of foliage originally planned for it and would benefit a great deal if the towers were lower or slightly farther apart, but one cannot help but marvel at the mothers hanging their clothes in the sun and the children playing undisturbed by passing vehicles.

Kiyonori Kikutake: Kata Housing System

One of the original members of the Metabolist Group and, along with Kurokawa its last remaining proponent, Kikutake has devoted considerable energy to the design of housing systems. Since Expo '70, where he displayed his aging Marina City models, Kikutake has developed what he calls the Kata Housing System. He explained that *kata* in Japanese can be written two ways: one form of *kanji,* 型 (Chinese-derived Japanese character), means a type, system or pattern; and the other *kanji,* 形 , means a figure or a model. The latter is sometimes pronounced *katachi,* meaning a shape or form. Both words employ the base *ka,* meaning image. According to Kikutake, his housing system is based, therefore, on a pattern or model which can adapt to different situations and develop a form or shape based on that particular situation. Although the polemic seems unnecessarily esoteric, the physical designs are interesting enough to warrant our attention.

The high-rise Tree Kata housing units are reminiscent of Kikutake's Marina City in

89

85–88.
Tree Kata Housing, Kiyonori Kikutake, 1972: One of the more interesting proposals developed by Kikutake in his continuing exploration of mass-housing prototypes. Still tainted with the blind idealism of the 60s, the various clusters suspended from a central core are beginning to lose their metabolic luster.
89.
Tiered Kata Housing, Kiyonori Kikutake, 1975: Finally built, this imaginative concept for tiered housing units falls far short of its European predecessors.

their placement on the site. Each is an individual tower connected only at the ground plane with its neighbors. Each tower is constructed of modular units arranged around a central core-shaft. These features alone seem to reiterate his earlier design concepts. To these familiar elements, Kikutake has added what he calls a "move-nette," which is a web of communal open spaces that weave through the complex, creating a network of communication and interaction places for people. This move-nette connects the high-rise towers with potential stepped elements

which can be inserted into the web at any elevation. The various models that Kikutake built are visually intriguing, but the details were never as clearly thought out nor as well articulated as they were in other proposals, such as the award-winning ASTM proposal for Ashiyahama.

The most recent and most convincing of Kikutake's Kata housing schemes is his Tiered Kata proposal—a well-conceived solution for housing people on Japan's hillsides without destroying the natural terrain. Better thought out than the Tree

Kata housing prototype, the Tiered Kata is still a far cry from the hillside-terraced housing of Europe, such as the Siedlung Halen or the Habitat at Berne by Atelier 5. Kikutake's terraced housing lacks the variety, spontaneity, and introduction of nature that Japanese residential architecture has traditionally achieved and that is essential to human habitation. Perhaps as he develops his system further, some of these necessary design features will appear.

Kenzo Tange & URTEC: New Urban Structuring Methods

In the 1970s, Kenzo Tange & URTEC began to reexamine the philosophies and concepts that led to the development of the Plan for Tokyo 1960. Certain concepts that still seem valid are being refined; other designs that now appear outdated are being replaced. The system of service cores and bridges, introduced by Isozaki in 1962, and realized by Tange at the Yamanashi Communications Center in 1966, is still being tested. The Communications Center itself is being expanded using a

very similar system to the one employed originally, while a variation of that concept is being explored in the design of Oran University in Algeria.

Oran University is designed to accommodate growth and change through a structure of vertical core-shafts and bridge elements forming academic clusters. Each cluster can expand out from a central spine of shaded communal space. The central spine is terminated by a tower which acts as the focus of campus activity. Oran University also explores the possibility of mixing the technologically derived

core-shaft system with more traditional building elements to achieve a variety and interest that was sometimes lacking in the megastructure schemes of the sixties.

Tange's most ambitious efforts in the seventies are in the area of new-town planning. The very name he has chosen for his firm expresses a commitment to urban design. In the late 1970s, the firm has been involved in the design of two sizeable new towns. One, called Hokusetsu, is proposed for an area north of the Japanese city of Kobe. It is being designed for a total population of 150,000. The other is called

91

92

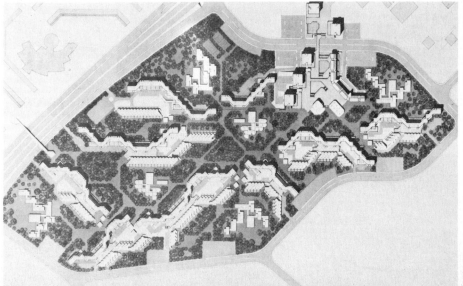

90.
Oran University, Kenzo Tange & URTEC, 1975: This university master plan integrates major green and public open spaces with the remnants of Tange's core shafts, first seen at the Yamanashi Communications Center. (See figure 37.)

91, 92.
Librino New Town, Kenzo Tange & URTEC, 1975: The master plan calls for a system of interlocking green spaces, with the park as the key structuring urban design element.

Librino New Town and is designed for a population of 60,000, to be located on the island of Sicily near the east-coast city of Catania.

Unlike the megastructures of 1960, both designs are much more sensitive to the need for integrating nature into urban environments. Tange explains that previously he was interested in a "very hard structure," but that now he is concerned with structuring the city by using "very soft communal spaces." This concept is illustrated in the master plan for Librino which is structured by a hierarchy of green spaces. There is a major green space surrounded by a meandering spine of minor green spaces. The minor green spine is further divided into residential clusters or communities, each with its local school and neighborhood shopping area. Each neighborhood is further connected to a central commercial and business center by a system of pedestrian and vehicular channels. Tange believes that many new-town designs lack urbanity and a sense of place. In order to achieve these vital qualities in Librino, he has created a system of pedestrian and vehicular streets that expand and contract in volume as one moves through them. The streets are set between high-rise and low-rise structures, allowing light and shadow to play on the changing surfaces. The varying widths are reminiscent of a European town in which narrow paths open up to pleasantly surprising piazzas, then shrink down again to nearly ordinary byways. Occasionally, the solid structure on one side of the street is split open, allowing a glimpse of the green spine.

Tange reminds us that before the industrial revolution, man had a positive contact with nature through his agriculture.

This was especially true among the rice paddies of Japan. Today, industrial man works with his mind and rarely has contact with nature. The basic concept underlying the design of Librino, Tange explains, is the desire to incorporate the stimulus of urbanity while simultaneously trying to "discover a new relationship between man and nature, a creative relationship."

As of this writing, Kenzo Tange & URTEC are involved in a systems approach to the design of the Japanese Archipelago, creating an integration of an energy system, an information system, a free-time system and a green network. One focus of their energies is the reevaluation of the Plan for Tokyo 1960, focusing on the green spine as a system of cultural communication spaces.

The Passing of an Era

The megastructures of the 1960s were the "Dinosaurs of the Modern Movement,"[28] as Reyner Banham affectionately labeled them. They were too big, too clumsy, and too inappropriate to the changing climate and environment for them to survive. As we entered the 1970s, the demise of the megastructure as the solution and panacea for all urban ills was clearly upon us. They were really never meant to be any more than conceptual prototypes to begin with, but when they began appearing in every architectural journal and every large-scale housing competition, it was necessary for someone to blow the whistle. Robert Venturi and Denise Scott Brown in late 1971 exclaimed:

"The world science futurist metaphysic, the megastructuralist mystique, and the look-Ma-no-buildings environmental suits and pods are a repetition of the mistakes of another generation. Their overdependence on a space age, futurist, or science fiction technology parallels the machine estheticism of the 1920's and approaches its ultimate mannerism. They are, however, unlike the architecture of the 1920's, artistically a dead end and socially a copout."[29]

By 1974, Jonathan Barnett in his pragmatic and inspired approach to urban design warned us further that:

"Designers have spent their time portraying cities as walking pods, spherical honeycombs, or endlessly spreading 'space frames'. Aside from the fact that such proposals ignore our existing inventory of cities, the social structure necessary to make such futurist visions work would be the most regressive imaginable."[30]

By 1976, megastructures were ancient history. Reyner Banham, who chronicled so carefully the rise and fall of the First Machine Age, was putting all the corpses to bed. In their epitaph he writes:

"To have the nerve to present such 'monumental follies,' as Peter Hall was to call them, seemed as natural in the mid-sixties as it must seem astounding today. But it must also, surely, seem intriguing, perhaps even exhilarating."

And finally he casts the megastructure aside as, "a whitening skeleton on the dark horizon of our recent architectural past."[31]

There developed in Japan during the seventies a certain "disillusionment with technology," according to Fumihiko Maki, which still exists today, because the dreams and visions of the early sixties did not produce the panacea they were proposing. However, Japanese architects are more realistic with respect to the potential and limitations of technology. The blind infatuation is passed, but the love affair lingers on. Urban design and architectural solutions continue to employ advanced technology when appropriate, rather than believing it will cure all of society's problems. The urban design solutions of the last ten years, including the work of Otaka, Otani and Tange, have been far more sensitive to their environments, more practical in terms of money, and more realistic about construction technology.

There remains, however, in Japan today a sense of optimism that the Japanese diligence and spirit will continue to uncover technological methods for solving at least some of the problems of tomorrow.

93.
Detail, Librino New Town: The hierarchy of scale from the low-rise to the high-rise housing blocks is articulated by the major green spine which links the residential zone to the commercial town center. Tange now believes the structuring of our cities should be based on the "soft, natural" elements, rather than the hard, permanent infrastructure of his earlier proposals.

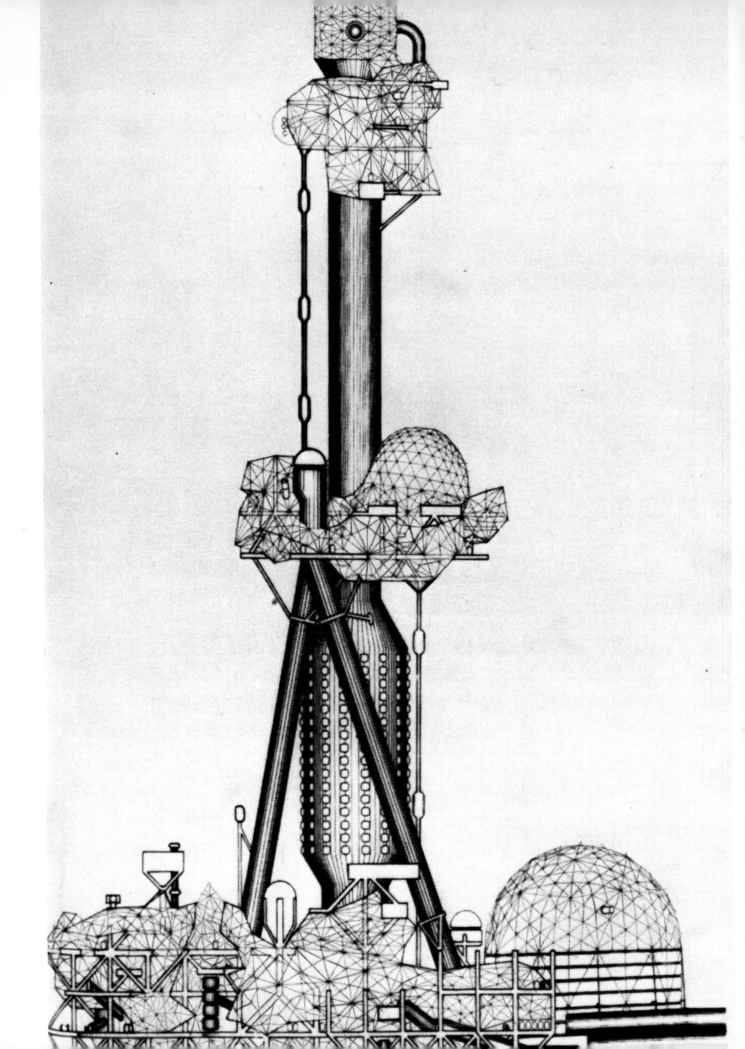

3.
Architechnology:
A New Integration of
Architecture and
Technology

During the early sixties a small group of dedicated, creative English architects got together and began producing a collection of extraordinary, futurist architectural proposals. They called themselves Archigram. Midway into the seventies a small group of dedicated, creative Japanese architects were doing their best to make such futurist schemes a reality.

Peter Cook's entertainment tower for the Montreal World Exposition of 1963 was realized, with minor alterations, at Expo '70 in Osaka through the efforts of Kiyonori Kikutake. Warren Chalk's imaginative Capsule Homes Tower of 1964 has its diminutive counterpart in the Kibogaoka Capsule Tower by Tatsuhiko Nakajima and GAUS (Institute of General Arts and Urban Sciences). And finally, the Archigram Instant City concept, proposed in 1969, of supporting temporary structures by suspending them from inflated balloons is being realized throughout Japan for festivals and other short-term facilities. These three examples are only a small indication of the fervor with which contemporary Japanese architects are working to realize the potential of a modular,

flexible architecture, first put forth only a decade ago.

The pressures to translate fantasy into concrete reality are probably greater in Japan than in any other industrialized country. An island nation with finite geographical limits, Japan is very densely populated. Both material and land costs are astronomical. Land in central Tokyo generally costs about $7 million per acre. Recently however, the Mitsubishi® Corporation paid an unprecedented and incredible $46 million per acre for a prime piece of Tokyo real estate.[32] Such exorbitant land and material costs, higher population densities, and an urgent postwar need for housing, combined with what Herman Kahn described as Japan's self-appointed task of, "catching up with or surpassing the West economically and technologically,"[33] have created a climate in which preindustrialized, prefabricated, and prepackaged building systems are flourishing on a scale unequalled in the Western world. This should come as no surprise to anyone acquainted with traditional Japanese construction, in which modular coordination and interchangeability of parts

are standard procedure. Bernard Rudofsky, author of Architecture Without Architects, has pointed out that:

"Centuries before we even thought of standardization, prefabrication and mobility as architectural possibilities, the Japanese applied them to their houses as a matter of course. From economical measures these developed to aesthetic norms. To enforce compliance of poor and rich in all matters of building, the authorities issued to the artisans precise specifications."[34]

As a nation very responsive to authority, these specifications were followed to the letter, and in time, walls, doors, windows, and floors became standardized in size and construction all over the country. It is understandable, therefore, that the modular coordination necessary for the successful industrialization of architecture was readily accepted. What is astounding however, is the diverse, unorthodox, yet remarkably creative way in which Japanese architects are borrowing, refining, and integrating industrial technology into contemporary architecture.

94.
Entertainment Tower for Montreal, Peter Cook, 1963: One of many visionary proposals from the Archigram group that found a receptive audience of admirers and imitators in Japan.

Closed versus Open Systems

Two approaches dominate the industrialization of building in Japan. One approach emphasizes economy, rationality, and limited interchangeability of parts. It may offer some variety in the planning stage, but once the layout is agreed to, the prefabricated pieces are interlocked into a closed unit. These projects are called "closed systems" because they accept only parts predesigned to fit into their closed universe. While most projects based on the closed-system principle are not very flexible, they are generally very efficient and sometimes ingenious in their ability to interlock components in a seemingly unending variety of ways, finally achieving a total unit reminiscent of a Japanese puzzle.

The second approach to industrialization is also the product of reason and logic, but utilizes a combination of separately prefabricated elements, each selected because of its capacity to serve a specific

95

95.
Expo '70 Tower, Kiyonori Kikutake, 1970: The geodesic domes clustered around the vertical core shaft were proof that Japanese architects had the technology and the courage to turn Archigram dreams into reality.
96.
Capsule Homes Tower, Warren Chalk, 1964: Another Archigram proposal; this one called for stacking preformed modules around a central core.
97.
Kibogaoka Youth Castle, Tatsuhiko Nakajima & GAUS, 1972: A diminutive version of Warren Chalk's Capsule Homes Tower, that was built outside Kyoto. (See figures 149–154, color plate 178.)

function. These are called "open systems." The basic concept here is greater flexibility for adapting to varying site conditions, functional requirements, and the changes incurred by time. To accept change easily, these structures are designed on the principle of Modularism, defined by Alvin Toffler as, "the attempt to lend whole structures greater permanence at the cost of making their substructures less permanent."[35] Thus, projects based on an open system begin as a neutral field into which a variety of clip-on, plug-in, snap-on, inflatable, unfoldable, detachable components can be forever rearranged to adapt to specific needs.

Among the plethora of closed systems being produced in Japan today, two projects emerge as representative of the best thinking in imaginative, efficient design. These are the MCS® (Mitsui Checker System), by the Mitsui Construction Company, and the TOS® (Taisei Overseas System), designed by Kisho Kurokawa and manufactured by the Taisei Construction Company. The MCS® employs precast-concrete members interlocked into a prefabricated steel superstructure. The name is derived from the precast planes that are interwoven into a "solid-void" or "checkered" pattern. This arrangement of precast members was found to be the most formidable in their ability to withstand earthquake tremors common in Japan. Another advantage of the checkered pattern is that it affords greater variety in floor-plan layout than the traditional shear wall system.

96

97

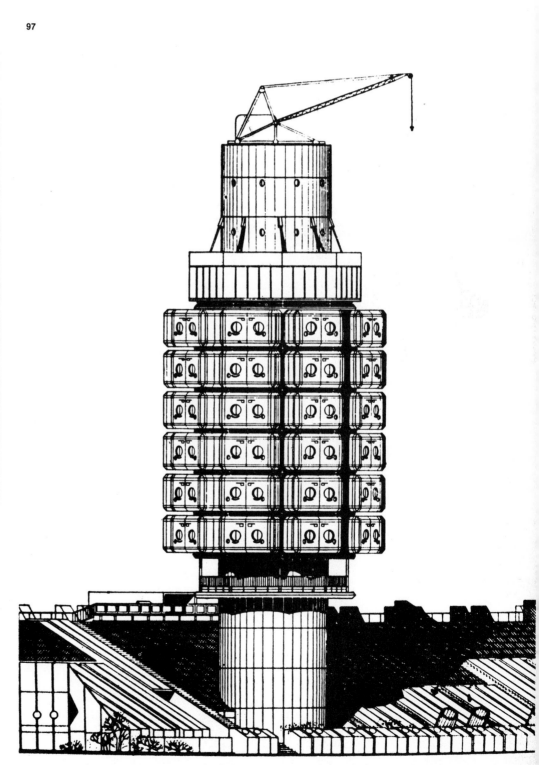

98

99

Recently, the MCS® has been employed to build Dezu New Town in Chiba Prefecture, one hour and twenty minutes by train from downtown Tokyo. Mitsui set up a precasting assembly line adjacent to the site of the new town in order to facilitate construction. A total of 1,412 living units were built in eight separate structures which have been designed to afford every unit maximum natural light all year. At the same time, the buildings have been shaped to create a vehicle-free park in the center of the complex. A typical two-bedroom unit with den (Japanese style) measures roughly 20 ft × 40 ft (6 m × 12 m) or 800 sq ft (72 m²). These units cost Mitsui about $15,000 each to construct in 1975 ($18.75/sq ft) and were sold as condominiums at $30,000 each. Even with an 80-minute commute to Tokyo, Mitsui representatives began construction confident of selling every unit before construction was completed, which they did.

By employing their own architects and engineers and by fabricating the building components adjacent to the construction site, Mitsui represents a model of other Japanese construction-company conglomerates that have cut costs substantially by putting research, development, design, and construction under one roof. While this system sometimes stifles the creative design that might be gained by hiring an independent architect, in the case of Mitsui, in-house designers give as much attention to intelligent space planning as they do to construction technology. Thus the final product is on a par with

100

98–100.
Dezu New Town, Mitsui Construction Company, 1974: Using the Mitsui Checker System, the interlocking precast concrete and steel structures can be erected quickly, at a cost of less than $20 per sq ft.
101.
Precasting Rig, Dezu New Town: Set on steel rails, this motorized device lifts precast panels from their casting beds and stacks them together. Later a crane mounted on rails will lift the concrete slabs into place.

101

the best closed systems being produced in the independent architectural offices.

The alternative to having designers in-house is to hire, on a consultant basis, an independent architect specializing in the creative application of industrialization to architecture. This is the story behind the Taisei Overseas System (TOS®). The Taisei Construction Company, contractors for many of the progressive pavillions at Expo '70 and a company with a long-standing interest in industrial technology,

hired Kisho Kurokawa, the champion of capsule architecture, to design a flexible, precast-concrete townhouse system. Kurokawa proposed a modular set of interlocking components to be arranged around a utility core in a three-dimensional matrix of almost infinite variation. All components are designed on a modular grid; the maximum dimension is determined by the Ministry of Transporation so that the units can be transported to any point in the country, or fit into containers and shipped to countries throughout

Southeast Asia where Taisei already has contracts committing them to the delivery of 500 units per year. In this way the closed-system building technology of Japan is beginning to solve the housing problem that is facing all of the developing nations of Asia.

While closed-system industrialized architecture inherently lacks the ability to change with time, it does offer variety in the planning stages and, considering the present state of the art, is the most eco-

102

103

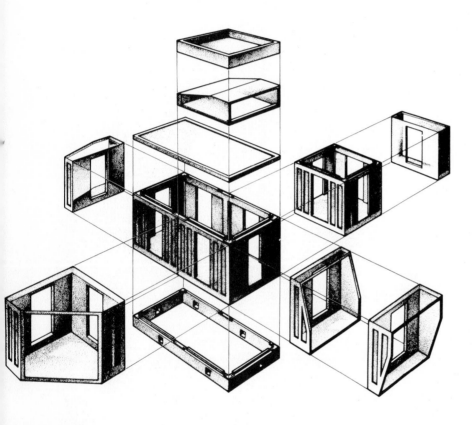

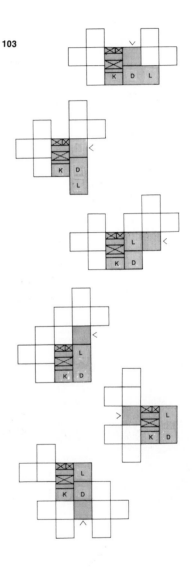

102, 103.
Taisei Overseas System, Design Prototype, Kisho Kurokawa, 1971: This closed system of prefabricated concrete elements fits together like the traditional Japanese puzzle. A variety of floor-plan clusters are available.
104.
Japanese Puzzle Instructions: The interlocking components form part of an ancient closed system familiar to all Japanese school children.

nomical, efficient way to build the repetitive components that make up most housing solutions. For these reasons, the Ministry of Construction in Japan has been sponsoring housing competitions focusing on middle- and high-rise developments, the most notable of these being the Pilot House and Ashiyahama projects. In both cases private industry is stimulated to produce a refined closed-system solution in the hopes of winning the competition, and with it a contract to build large portions of a new community.[36]

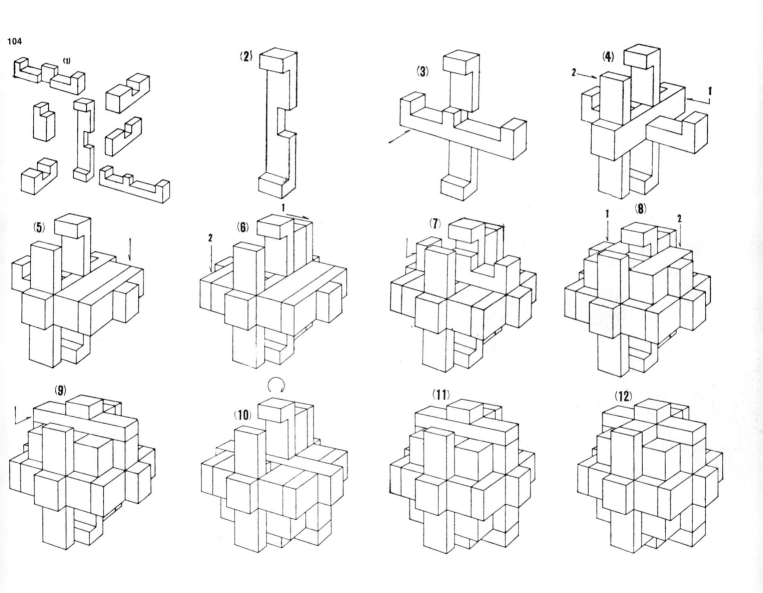

Open Systems

Beyond the precision and efficiency of all closed systems, is the question that has haunted every hot-rod designer since the beginning of the industrial revolution: why won't a Ford engine drop neatly into a Chevy chassis? Any architect who has sat laboriously counting brick courses or paid exorbitant fees to watch a skilled laborer saw concrete blocks to fit his wonderful design must at some point ask the same kind of question: "why can't all the separately manufactured pieces fit neatly to-

gether?" The answer to this question is the dream of the "open-system" designer. The man in Japan who is devoted to making this dream a reality is Professor Yoshichika Uchida of Tokyo Universty.

Professor Uchida's Architectural Technology Laboratory focuses on the analysis of industrialized building systems from all over the world. Based on their findings, the Laboratory proposes new systems integrating and improving on the concepts previously put forth. Recently the emphasis of the Laboratory has been on the de-

velopment of a viable open system of industrialized construction. Professor Uchida believes that such a system should flourish easily in Japan because her traditional architecture is itself a form of open system;

"It is well known that Japanese traditional houses are characterized by the use of wood, the planning on grid, both horizontal and vertical, and the post-and-beam construction. That Japan has a traditional module system is of the utmost importance in relation to the 'open' system. . . .

105

106

107

108

110

111

105, 106.
Taisei Overseas System, 1973: Prototypical box units are carried on flatbed trucks and set in place by two men.
107–109.
Taisei Overseas System: Model variations represent only three of the many configurations available using this flexible system of modular components.

109

110.
The ancient art of weaving *tatami* straw mats is still practiced today, even on the side streets of urban Tokyo. The rectangular (90 cm × 180 cm, approximately 3 ft × 6 ft) mat composed of a double square, forms the basic module of all Japanese homes.
111.
The traditional Japanese wooden house reveals post-and-beam construction and an open system of interchangeable components using the ancient grid measurement of one *shaku* (30 cm, or about one foot).
112–113.
GUP VII, Uchida Laboratory, Tokyo University, 1972: This open-system proposal employs a flexible structural skeleton combined with a variety of box units.
114.
GUP VII: Built into this kitchen box unit is the "hot panel" containing piping and conduit for appliances.

It may well be said that no traditional building practice in the world has ever given birth to more 'open' components than that of Japan. For example, we have tatami, *or a 90 cm* × *180 cm straw mat,* shoji, *or a sliding screen covered with translucent paper, and* fusuma, *or a sliding screen with [opaque] paper glued on both sides, and so on. Above all,* fusuma *and* shoji *are the traditional building components that exceptionally satisfy the contemporary qualifications for the open component.''* [37]

With the confidence that Japan is fertile ground for implanting the seeds of open-systems architecture, the Uchida Laboratory has been producing a series of open-system proposals, one of the most interesting of which is the GUP VII (Group Uchida Project No. 7) housing system. Based loosely on Le Corbusier's famous idea of slipping a prefabricated box into a frame, the Uchida group has blown open the sides of the box as well as the structural skeleton itself, lending far more flexibility to the system.

Remembering that the basic premise of open-systems architecture is to create a neutral field into which any combination of prefabricated components can be inserted, GUP VII employs an erector-set series of structural components which clip together leaving a regular grid of voids and shafts for mechanical equipment which can be replaced easily without disassembling the structure itself. The mechanical equipment is also designed as an open-ended set of prefabricated panels, shafts, and units which are slid easily into

112

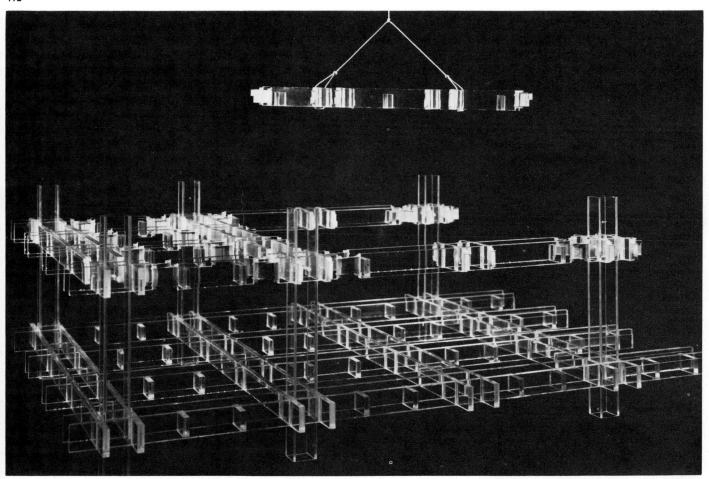

113

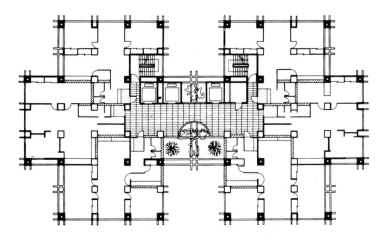

114

the structural skeleton. Kitchen and sanitary units, for example, are backed up against what Uchida calls a ''hot panel''— a panel containing racks of pipes and conduits—which can be replaced much in the same manner a computer circuit is snapped into your TV set.

The remainder of GUP VII is comprised of ''box units.'' These units are inserted into the skeleton, then interlocked and cantilevered in a wide variety of configurations. Unlike Le Corbusier's Unité d'Habitation in which each unit was uncomfortably squeezed into a 12-ft × 80-ft (3.7-m × 24-m) shoe box, GUP VII offers the potential to expand up, down or sideways. The system is even flexible enough to negotiate steep slopes and uneven terrain. Since the box units and the structural skeleton are independently self-supporting, it is possible to create two- and three-story spaces simply by not inserting a number of box units.

The entire open system is designed on a grid based on the standard Japanese dimension of one *shaku* (30 cm), or about one foot. The basic box unit is roughly 9 ft × 12 ft. A typical apartment may be comprised of six or seven boxes, roughly 700 sq ft (65 m²) combined with the 3 ft (90 cm) of space between units; this totals about 1,100 sq ft (102 m²).

Professor Uchida's Laboratory has also proposed open systems in which the box unit itself is the supporting structure, which eliminates the need for an indepen-

115

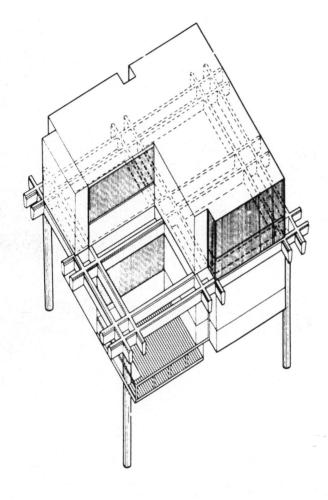

116

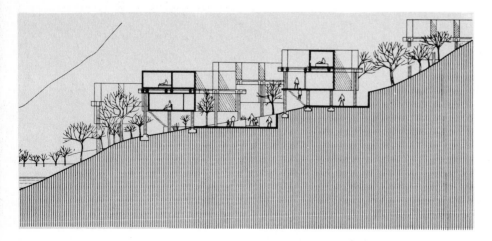

117

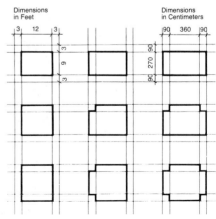

dent structural skeleton. At present however, the open-system idea which has the greatest chance of succeeding in Japan is the box-unit concept proposed and detailed in the GUP VII system.

The student most directly responsible for the development of GUP VII was Katsuhiko Ohno, who received his Doctor of Engineering degree from the Uchida Laboratory in April, 1972. Since that time the prodigious Dr. Ohno has convinced the Sekisui® Chemical Company to produce a slightly simplified version of the box-unit open system. The Uchida Laboratory studies industrialized building methods so thoroughly that it is possible for a graduating student to apply his new knowledge directly to real situations.

The Sekisui® Chemical Co. has named the box-unit system Sekisui Haim®. Production began early in 1973, in two separate factories with an annual estimated output of 40,000 box units. The factories are set up like automobile assembly plants and at optimum efficency produce 100 units per day per factory. In an eight-hour day, that equals 12.5 units per hour, or 1.0 unit every five minutes. Each unit weighs 1½ to 2 tons and costs about $3,000. The units are constructed of a light-gauge steel frame with steel and wood infill panels. A typical three-bedroom house comprised of seven or eight units can be erected in no more than three hours, not including caulking and finishing. The completed house, with built-in wall storage units sells for about $25,000.

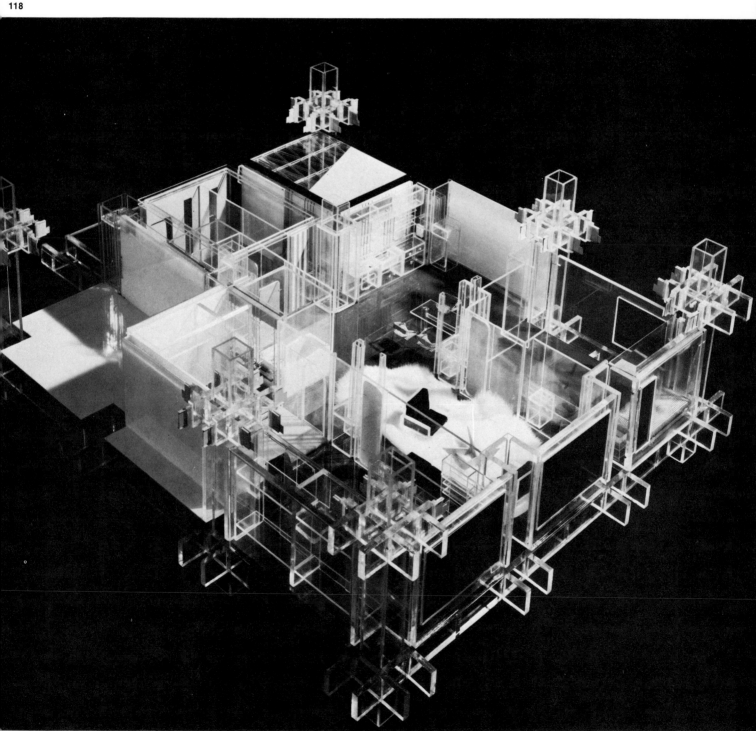

The Sekisui® Chemical Company is now offering the box-unit house in 20 variations, and as technology becomes more sophisticated the options will expand, until it is possible to offer people architectural choices of enormous variety at an economical price. This phenomenon has been asserted by several observers of superindustrial society, notably Alvin Toffler, who claimed that:

"The more advanced the technology, the cheaper it is to introduce variation in output. We can safely predict, therefore, that when the construction industry catches up with manufacture in technological sophistication, gas stations, airports and hotels, as well as supermarkets, will stop looking as if they had been poured from the same mold. Uniformity will give way to diversity."[38]

Marshall McLuhan has further pointed out that:

"When automated electronic production reaches full potential, it will be just as cheap to turn out a million differing objects as a million exact duplicates. The only limits on production and consumption will be the human imagination."[39]

This ability to harness advanced technology in order to offer more permutations and variations in building systems is already becoming apparent in Japan. Apart from Sekisui Haim®, the box-unit housing concept is being expanded and refined by the Shinihon Steel Company, the Yawata

119

120

121

119.
Sekisui Haim®, Katsuhiko Ohno, 1973: The
manufacturing plant, modeled after an automobile
assembly line, produces one box unit every five
minutes.
120, 121.
Sekisui Haim®: A typical three-bedroom house
employing seven or eight box units can be assembled
in three hours, not including foundations, caulking
and finishing.

Steel Company, and a host of others bent on fulfilling the promise of open-system flexibility.

Another company determined to advance the technology of housing construction is Misawa Homes. A prefabricated-housing company started in 1962 by Chiyoji Misawa as an offshoot of his family's lumber company, Misawa Homes increased its sales in 1970 to $83 million, a 95% increase over 1969, and a 166% increase in net earnings. Misawa Homes has una-bashedly modeled its entire operational hierarchy on the automobile industry, using three basic phases: production, sales, and construction. Production is defined as, "the process involving the research, development, and manufacture of products."[40] This is where Misawa focuses their energy. The sale of their products is handled by franchised dealers (20 in Japan), and the construction is done by bon-afide contractors (1,200 throughout the country). By using the automobile industry as a model, Misawa has managed to serve an enormous market while focusing solely on the design and prefabrication of building components.

With no qualms about borrowing exper-tise from other sectors of Japan's indus-trial base, Misawa enlisted the services of Tadashi Hanaoka, a talented industrial de-signer who had been previously employed by automobile manufacturers Isuzu® of Japan and Ghia® of Italy. Intent on bring-ing the diversity of choice and the sophis-tication of mass-production technology to

122

123

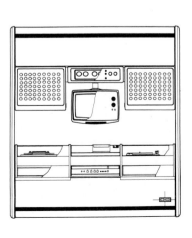
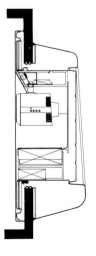

124

the housing industry, Hanaoka has proposed a series of plug-in wall units, These include an environmental control unit and an electronic communication unit, as well as sanitary, culinary and dressing units. A radical departure from most industrialized housing schemes which generally assemble the mechanical functions into a compact core, Hanaoka believes that the rapidly evolving mechanical technology which serves the living spaces should be more easily accessible and adaptable to change, and has therefore distributed his plug-in wall units around the periphery of the building. Each unit contains a modular set of appliances and equipment which can be updated easily. At the same time it is possible to simply remove the entire unit and replace it with a different or improved model. In other words it is not only possible to unplug the entire unit, it is even possible, and economically feasible, to unplug pieces of the piece. This is a confirmation of Toffler's dictum that, "as technology becomes more sophisticated, the cost of introducing variation declines."[41]

122–125.
Misawa Homes Wall Units, Tadashi Hanaoka, 1973: These clip-on, preindustrialized units include an environmental control unit (122); a communications unit (123); a culinary unit (124); and a sanitary unit (125).

126.
Shinihon Steel Company, 1973: One of the many prefabricated box units being produced in Japan, this one slides into a rectangular structural frame, just as Le Corbusier envisioned in 1947.

127.
Prefabricated Cell, Unité d'Habitation, Le Corbusier, 1947: This prophetic conceptual model of prefabricated living "cells," as Corbu called them, was never implemented in his masterpiece at Marseilles, but has been reincarnated and is thriving in a wide variety of forms today in Japan.

126

125

127

The wall units are constructed of vacuum-formed FRP (fiber-reinforced plastic) so as to be resistant to the highest wind loads and earthquake tremors. In addition, special tubing has been implanted throughout the unit's casing so that it is both sound- and water-proofed. When installed, the units cantilever from the building so as not to infringe on valuable interior living spaces. All piping, ductwork, and electrical conduit is located within the units themselves. This facilitates servicing and renders the units almost self-sufficient. This is one of the key qualities of a well-designed open-system component; that it is, in effect, an independent entity and can be introduced into an architectural framework, or detached from it, without disturbing the basic functions of the framework itself.

Components that meet these open-system specifications are now being manufactured in Japan in ever-increasing numbers. Interlocking box units, culinary, sanitary, and environmental control modules, as well as unfolding garages, inflatable living rooms, and premolded plastic capsules, are all available right out of the catalogue. Charles Eames' dream of being able to select open components from a catalogue and integrate them into a flexible environment for living, as he attempted to do in his Pacific Palisades home in 1949, has more than ever become a reality in the world's fastest growing superindustrial state. With 90% of all Japanese housing designed on a 90-cm module (about 3 ft.), the flexibility, adaptability, and interchangeablility of parts inherent in open systems are creating an industrialized architecture of unlimited variety.

128

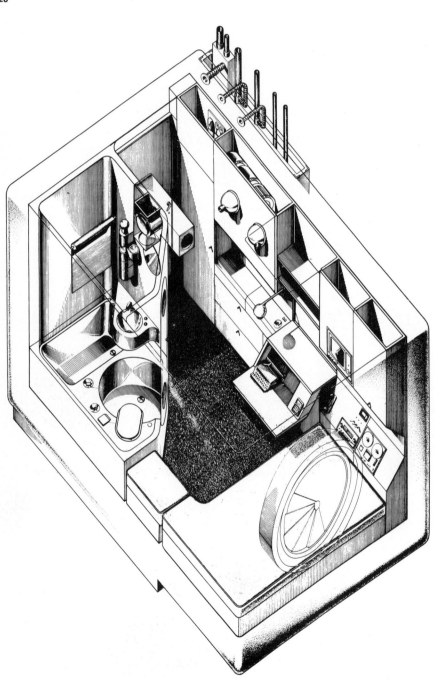

128–130.
Nakagin Capsule Building, Kisho Kurokawa, 1972: The Nakagin capsule, based on outer-space precedents, is a total living environment attached to a service core. In a space approximately 8 ft × 12 ft, Kurokawa has adroitly organized a complete bathroom, double bed, HVAC (Heating, Ventilating and Air Conditioning) unit, desk, chair, storage space and convertible kitchen area. Equivalent to a standard six-*tatami*-mat room, this small area is not uncommon for bachelors and some young married couples in dense Japanese cities. (See figure 56.)

129

Kisho Kurokawa: Capsules and Mixed Systems

The term "industrialized building" most often generates images of prefabricated boxes or interlocking planes organized on a modular coordination grid. These mental images are the result of the open- and closed-systems buildings that are proliferating around the globe. At the same time that these open and closed systems are being developed and refined, a quiet revolution is occurring in "architechnology"—architecture utilizing industrial technol-ogy—that could restructure our urban environments. Largely under the influence of aerospace hardware, architects are designing space capsules that do everything but fly. By far the most influential proponent of capsule architecture is Kisho Kurokawa. His interest in architechnology dates back as far as 1959, when Kurokawa published a book on industrialized housing in the Soviet Union, written after extensive travels through that country. Since that time his interest in industrialization has evolved from his box-form mass housing in 1962, through his Celestial Theme Pavilion and Takara Beautilion at Expo '70, to his present focus on the capsule.

Like the aerospace industry from which the term was borrowed, Kurokawa has designed his capsules to be miniuniverses. In his Nakagin Capsule Building, man is offered a complete living environment in a space no more than 8 ft × 12 ft (2.4 m × 3.8 m). Carefully packaged into this small volume is a bathroom with Japanese-style bathtub, an HVAC unit, double bed, desk, chair, storage space, TV, tapedeck, typewriter, desk calculator, clock radio, and

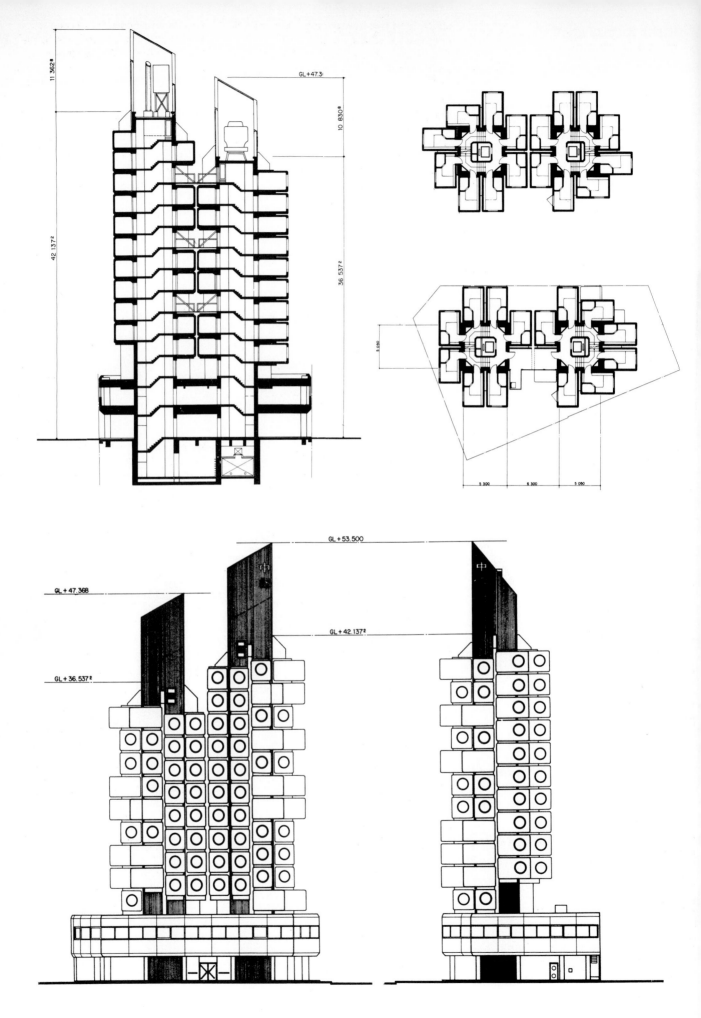

space for a two-burner stove. A more efficient use of space would be difficult to find even in densely packed Tokyo. The main objective of capsule architecture, claims Kurokawa, is to achieve "one hundred percent mass production of living units by creating a new understanding of the house as a community of individuals." The Nakagin Capsule Building represents the first link in such an architectonic community; one that would be composed of towers of variable heights interconnected by pedestrian bridges, with personalized capsules clustered around each tower.

To achieve such a community of individuals it is necessary to give life to the capsule by joining it to a mother-ship that will provide the water, oxygen, and power supply essential for its functioning. This need generated a system of construction that combines prefabricated components with the more familiar elements of traditional construction. We call these "mixed systems." The Nakagin Capsule Building is a perfect example. It employs two steel-frame, reinforced-concrete towers that act as public space-shafts servicing the individual rooms. These service towers form

132

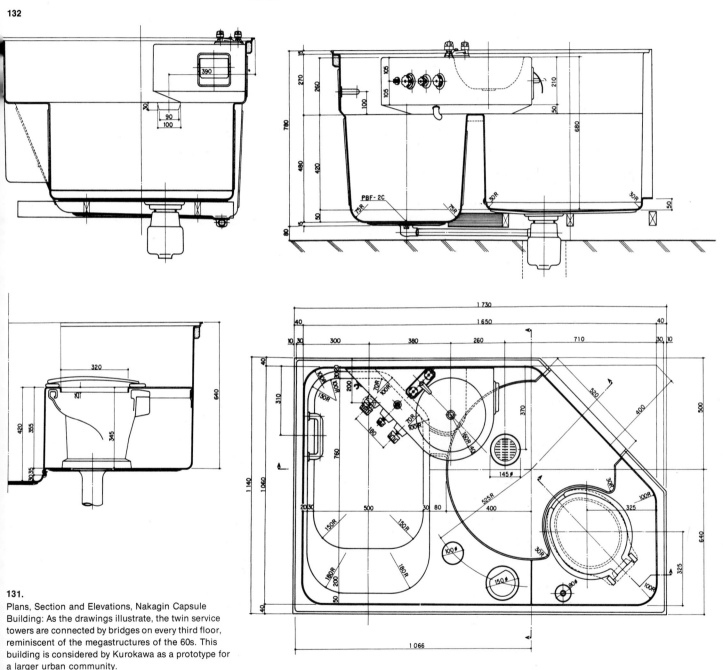

131.
Plans, Section and Elevations, Nakagin Capsule Building: As the drawings illustrate, the twin service towers are connected by bridges on every third floor, reminiscent of the megastructures of the 60s. This building is considered by Kurokawa as a prototype for a larger urban community.
132.
Bathroom, Nakagin Capsule: Evolved from the toilet capsules that Kurokawa created for the Celestial Theme Pavilion at Expo '70, this piece of industrial design is in itself a modern-day Japanese puzzle, integrating all sanitary functions into 21 sq ft (2m²).

133.
Nakagin Capsule: The lightweight steel truss box being welded together by the same firm that manufactures shipping containers.
134–136.
Capsule Technology: Based on the innovative Japanese shipping and railroad container industry, the Nakagin capsule is produced on the same rig as the JNR (Japan National Railway) container in the foreground (136) and can be transported all over the world using existing shipping-container technology (134) and flatbed trucks (135).

133

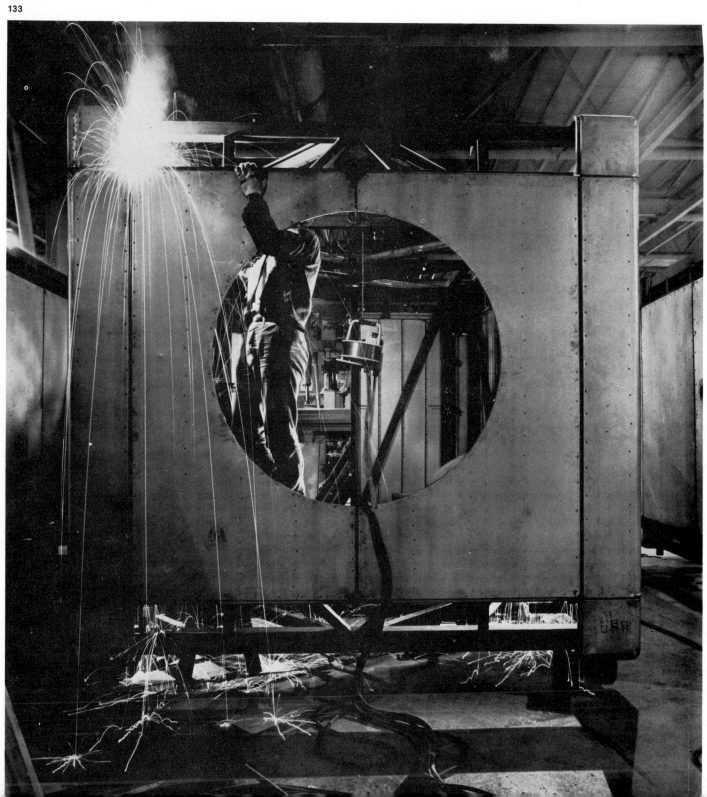

the structural trunks as well as housing the elevators, staircases, and vertical racks of piping. The towers are linked together by bridges forming what Kurokawa believes is a kind of megastructure that could act as a framework for the multilevel city of the future. By mixing traditional construction techniques with industrialized, interchangeable components, Kurokawa has created a mixed-systems architecture that is perhaps even more flexible than the present open systems which accept only prefabricated components. The virtue of a mixed system is that the architect is no longer restricted to one technology, but can aggregate, synthesize, and amalgamate elements of technology from a broad, industrial base. The Nakagin capsule is itself a case in point. The basic structure is an all-welded, light-weight, steel box, manufactured by Aruna Koki on an improved version of the same rig they use to produce large shipping containers. By tapping the expertise of the largest shipbuilding nation in the world, the one who pioneered containerization for transoceanic freight, Kurokawa has fused two technologies, affirming the versatility of mixed-systems architecture. Just as the containers are transported by rail and truck all over Japan, it is now equally possible for factory-finished capsules to reach anywhere in the country, or in the world for that matter. Accordingly, Mr. Kurokawa is now negotiating with contractors in England and in San Francisco who are interested in building capsule towers of their own. This is not surprising when one considers that the completed capsule with all the furnishings and appliances costs no more than a Toyota® Corolla.

134

136

135

The over-all building aesthetic is that of a complex, interlocking puzzle. This inter-penetrating solid-void effect is reminiscent of traditional Japanese wood-block puzzles in which a series of similar, precut elements are carefully fit together to form the total image. This aesthetic system dates back to the early Buddhist pagodas and temple architecture of the seventh century, in which predesigned wooden members were interlocked forming the multiple bracketing structures that we

137

138

139

137–139.
Nakagin Capsule Building: The aesthetic system employed by Kurokawa (139) is clearly based on the familiar Japanese puzzle of interlocking components (138), which is itself descended from the ancient wood bracketing systems found in Japanese temple architecture (137), exhibiting the unique ability to be both innovative and traditional simultaneously.
140, 141.
LC-30X Leisure Capsule, Isometric, Plan and Prototypical Unit, Kisho Kurokawa, 1972: A logical evolution of the Nakagin capsule, this capsule cluster combines a service module, sleeping module and living module.

have come to identify with Japan. The present aesthetic, borrowed from the past yet employing contemporary components, has penetrated the modern movement in Japanese architecture. Similar influences can be found in the post-Metabolist architecture of Kenzo Tange, Masato Otaka, Sachio Otani, and Kiyonori Kikutake.

The ability to mix technologies and to combine seemingly divergent and contrasting parts into an integrated whole is the key to Japan's success in the field of industrialized architecture. The Nakagin Capsule Building, completed in 1972, was the beginning of an investigation into mixed systems which is still very much alive today. Leading the development of these new systems is none other than Kisho Kurokawa himself. The Nakagin capsule, although remarkably well detailed, is in the final analysis, a somewhat confined space. To remedy this situation

Kurokawa has developed the LC-30X leisure capsule, which is, in effect, a cluster of capsules. Like its interplanetary antecedents, the LC-30X capsule is divided into functional modules, including a service module, a sleeping module, and a living or leisure module. These modules can be arranged in several configurations.

The structure of the capsule is a rigid frame made of quarter-round, rolled steel 3.2 mm (0.13 in) thick. These rigid units

140

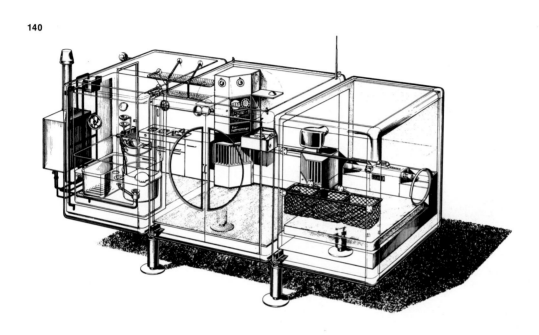

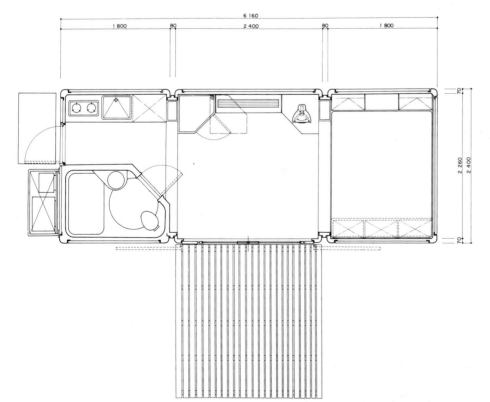

141

are designed to be inserted into a super-space frame which can be free standing or can be anchored into a hill. Presently design development is proceeding for a hill community to be constructed near Usami on the Izu peninsula. One of the main objectives of this project is to use the sophistication of technology while maintaining the natural slope of the site. By having vehicular traffic enter the site at specified levels, residents of the community can walk down a sloped path to their leisure capsule, which achieves an ecological

balance that is rare in industrialized housing today.

In yet another attempt to integrate contrasting elements, Kurokawa has designed his capsule house in Karuizawa. Utilizing mixed-systems architecture, the house is made up of four Corten® steel capsules suspended from a miniature concrete tower. The exterior is strictly "high-tech," while the interior has a surprisingly warm, woody, residential atmosphere. Functionally the capsules are divided into two

142

142, 143.
LC-30X Leisure Capsule: Plans for this leisure capsule include several hillside resorts and the potential for a diagonal, truss-supported megastructure.
144, 145.
Karuizawa House, Kisho Kurokawa, 1974: This country retreat is a miniature Nakagin Capsule Building employing a concrete core as living room and studio with Corten® steel capsules suspended from it.

143

145

144

sleeping modules (each with private bath), one culinary capsule, and one tea-ceremony capsule. The interiors of these capsules vary enormously to fit their specific purposes. The culinary capsule appliances incorporate all the latest in electronic and hydraulic technology, whereas the tea-ceremony capsule is copied directly from the famous Tea Master, Masakazu Kobori usually known as Enshu Kobori (1579–1647). Kurokawa is an ar-

dent student of Enshu Kobori, who is perhaps best known for the elegant Tea House at Katsura Detached Palace, outside Kyoto. The interior of the capsule tea house accordingly includes the required four-and-one-half *tatami* (straw mats) floor; the *shoji* screens; the *chigaidana,* or uneven shelves, and the *tokonoma* (alcove). The use of a prefabricated, rust-red, Corten® steel capsule to house a tea-ceremony room, true in every respect to its

seventeenth-century counterpart, may strike adherents of Bauhaus principles as lacking integrity, but it exemplifies beautifully the unique Japanese ability to use contrary elements together to create what we call Both/And architecture. It is prevalent throughout the country and represents the generating principle behind the rapidly developing mixed-systems industrialized architecture of Japan.

146

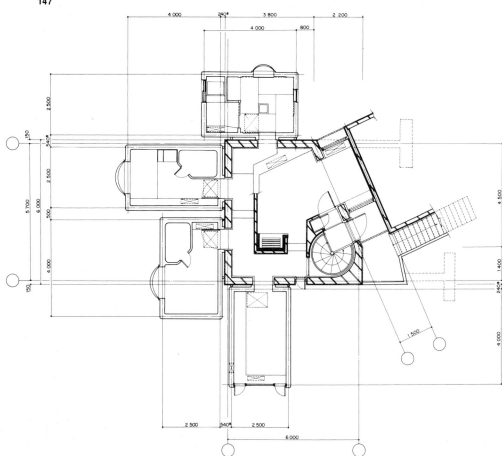

146.
Interior, Karuizawa House: In bold contrast to the high-tech exterior, Kurokawa has created a warm and woody country-house interior. The traditional Tea Ceremony Room with *shoji* screens and *tatami* mats is visible in the background.

147, 148.
Plans, Karuizawa House: Off the central core, Kurokawa has arranged a culinary capsule, two Nakagin-like sleeping modules, and a Tea Ceremony Room within the Corten® steel capsule. This ability to combine contrary elements into an integrated whole creates the Both/And architecture unique to Japan.

148

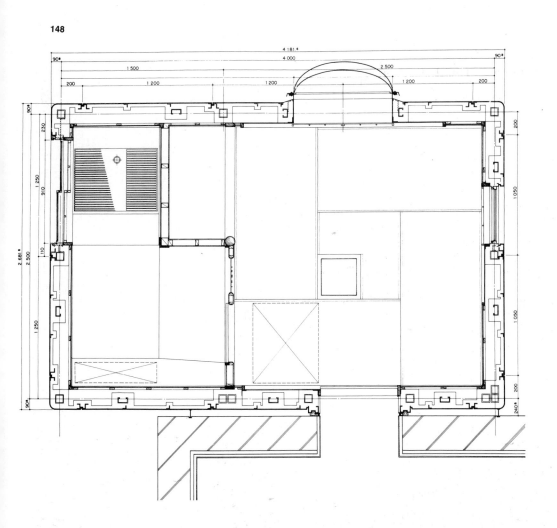

Nakajima & GAUS: Mixed Systems Capsule Castle

One of the finest examples of this architectural trend is the Kibogaoka Youth Castle in Shiga Prefecture, designed by Tatsuhiko Nakajima & GAUS (Institute of General Arts and Urban Sciences). According to Mr. Nakajima, the highly diverse structure was meant to act as a visual focus as well as a symbol of technological progress for the residents of Shiga Prefecture. It does both successfully. The open arms of the plan receive approaching guests while the capsule

tower draws their attention across the 2,000-acre (810-hectare) cultural park. This expansive area is divided into three zones: sports, outdoor activities, and culture. The entire park acts as a green belt between two urban centers, Keihanshin and Chukyo, while the Youth Castle forms the nucleus of the culture zone.

The building itself is an intriguing assemblage of preindustrialized components, each one serving a specific function. The dominant element is of course the capsule tower, made up of a reinforced-concrete cylinder which supports and services the

nine capsules clustered around it at each level. The capsules themselves are, in effect, sleeping and study modules and, unlike the Nakagin capsules, are not equipped with private bath. Instead, a separate service capsule has been included on each floor to provide necessary plumbing facilities, thereby limiting piping to a very finite area. The capsules are constructed of bent and grooved steel plates braced inside the premolded walls. They are suspended from the cylindrical core in a most interesting manner. Arranged radially, they were supported at first by cantilevered concrete beams connected by

149

150

149, 150.
Kibogaoka Youth Castle, Tatsuhiko Nakajima & GAUS,
1972: A visual focus for Shiga Prefecture, a mountain
resort and an assemblage of prefabricated components. The premolded FRP (fiber-reinforced plastic)
capsules are clustered around a concrete core shaft.
(See figure 97, color plate 178.)
151.
Interior, Kibogaoka Youth Castle: East meets West as a
copy of Michelangelo's David graces the front lobby
along with HVAC units resembling Saturn Five rocket
boosters, and canvas-wrapped, sanitary modules
suspended from the walls.

steel rods running from the top of the major cylinder. After all the capsules were in place, post-tensioning was introduced by means of an oil jack located at the top of the tower. In this way the capsules are supported simultaneously by compression and tension, which according to the designers, will withstand the irregular vertical and horizontal forces of earthquakes.

In counterpoint to the vertical tower is the variegated horizontal space of the City Tube. According to Akira Shibuya,[42] one of the project architects at GAUS, the City Tube was designed to bring the diversity and stimulation of urban space to this focus of cultural activity. The expanding and contracting spaces of the City Tube are unified by a space-frame roof covered with a glass sandwich panel filled with mineral-wool fiber. This preindustrialized roofing system insulates the space while filling it with bright, natural light. Punctuating the linear space are sanitary capsules wrapped in translucent canvas, prepackaged stainless steel HVAC units, and a visitor information/security control station. Sculptural elements on opposite sides of the City Tube are men's and women's public baths consisting of preformed FRP (fiber-reinforced plastic) shells set on their side. These shells bring a warm, natural light into the rooms while at the same time assure visual privacy.

As a total entity the multifarious Kibogaoka Youth Castle is an imposing structure; yet, within the bold framework there is an intelligent application of technology to architecture. Industrialized building components have been used as a vehicle for expression, but at the same time are

152

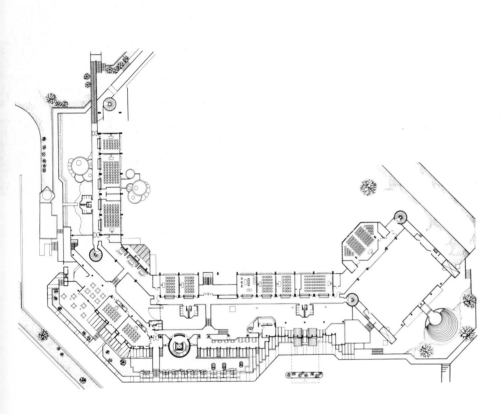

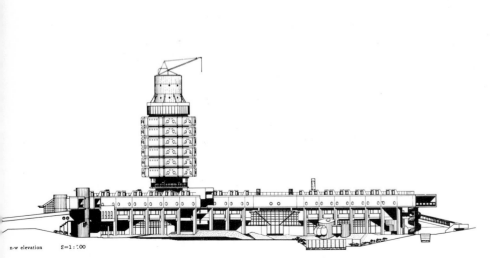

153

154

152.
Elevation and Plan, Kibogaoka Youth Castle: The City Tube, or internal space, is a lively mixture of skylights, preindustrialized components, and sculptural elements arranged to heighten the spatial sequence.
153, 154.
Detail, Kibogaoka Youth Castle: The bulging cupolas on the side of the building are a cluster of FRP domes which give visual privacy to the public baths within, while bathing the space in warm, natural light.
155.
Yamazaki House No. 1, Yoji Watanabe, 1962: While the Metabolist movement was in high gear, Watanabe was still having a nostalgic affair with traditional Japanese wood and stucco building materials.
156.
Plan, New Sky Building No. 3, Yoji Watanabe, 1967: After acquiring a taste for the techno-aesthetic, Watanabe developed his New Sky Building series as futurist fantasies dressing traditional Japanese rooms in a facade of technology.

serving the human beings that inhabit the capsules and meeting rooms within the building. The facility of employing industrial components in juxtaposition to each other as well as with traditional building elements, as was achieved in Kibogaoka, is the promise of mixed-systems architecture. The research and refinement of these building systems that has produced so much already, is continuing at GAUS, at the Tokyo University Uchida Laboratory, at the Kisho Kurokawa office, and at Tatsuhiko Nakajima's new firm, HB. According to his partner, Masako Akamatsu,

the name HB was derived from the type of pencil lead which is, "not hard and not soft," but rather "a combination of various elements." This might, in fact, be an ample definition for the entire movement.

The Techno-Aesthetic: A Facade of Technology

Among the many architects responding to the influences of industry on architectural design, there are some who are more concerned with the visual product than with the construction techniques of building.

This has produced a school of thought that embraces the image of technology: the "techno-aesthetic." This aesthetic emphasis is creating buildings that look like pieces of technology, rather than buildings that incorporate industrial principles into their construction. This is not unlike the "experience makers" of the automobile and electronics industries who increase the number of dials and gadgets on a product to give the user the sense of being master of a complex piece of technology.[43] It is this psychological payoff that is stressed more than the pragmatic

155

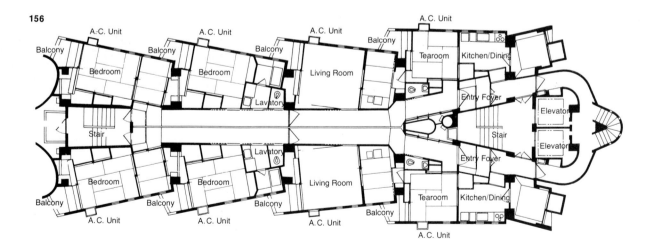

156

functioning of the product. The application of this concept to architecture, while visually amusing, is fraught with grave implications. It is essential that as architects we distinguish between visual preoccupations and the intelligent application of technology to building.

In Japan the man probably most fascinated by the techno-aesthetic is Yoji Watanabe, a relative newcomer to the use of industrialized components in architecture. During the 1960s when the Metabolist movement was at its height, seeking to find new ways of relating technological change to human habitation and the burgeoning of cities, Mr. Watanabe was still immersed in a nostalgic affair with traditional Japanese materials and forms. This is apparent in his Yamazaki House No. 1 in which he played with interlocking wooden structural members and employed traditional interior building elements. Since that time he has acquired a taste for the "image-of-the-machine," the techno-aesthetic, which is, both literally and metaphorically, a facade of technology. This was first demonstrated in the now-famous New Sky Building No. 3, in which Watanabe dressed traditional Japanese interiors with imitation "Airstream" mobile homes stacked one upon the other. Although these units resemble capsules, they are merely the prefabricated facade, and not an integration of advanced technology with a service tower as in the Nakagin Capsule Building and in the Kibogaoka Youth Castle. As to the streamlined water tanks on the roof, Watanabe explained that he was "influenced by the desire to recreate the marine architecture of the Navy," in which he was a lieutenant.

This preoccupation with the machine aesthetic has continued to permeate Watanabe's recent work. In his design for the New Sky Building No. 5, he attempted to create a sleek object with "exhaust pipes" for "dragging" down the street. His aesthetic concept is clearly represented in his model for the building, which is made of sheet aluminum, although the actual reinforced-concrete structure bears little resemblance to the conceptual ideal.

One of his more recently completed works is the Doctor Yamazaki Residence No. 2

(not the same Yamazaki for whom Watanabe designed the traditional house a decade earlier). The building seems to be four capsules suspended from a core, but in reality is another reinforced-concrete hoax, straining the traditional material to its limits. When I visited the building with the architect, I mentioned this apparent paradox. He explained that it was "a harmonious combination between traditional Japan and the modern West." Later in discussing a housing competition entry of his, I asked how he felt about using systems analysis in his work, either in the

159.

158.

157.
New Sky Building No. 3: An aluminum-clad spaceship with a "control tower" based on the submarine architecture of Watanabe's navy days. (See color plate 188.)

158, 159.
New Sky Building No. 5, Yoji Watanabe, 1971: As the silvery study model indicates (159), this was to be another of Watanabe's wonderful pieces of fantasy architecture. As finally constructed in concrete (158) it is a sad shell of its former self.

programming and design phases or in the construction phase. Mr. Watanabe replied that, "The Japanese architect tries to distinguish himself from engineers or technical specialists. He considers himself more or less close to an artist or a philosopher. Any architect who depends on computers is a poor architect." This reconfirmed Mr. Watanabe's devotion to the aesthetics of technology, even to the exclusion of actual technological advancement itself.

Clearly every architect is charged with the responsibility of creating visually stimulating environments, and whether his preference is for Classical, Mannerist, or Baroque architecture is his personal choice; but to confuse an infatuation with the image-of-the-machine and its resultant visual formalism, with the substantial development of architectural technology is a serious trap into which we must avoid being seduced.

In retrospect, I remain an admirer of Mr. Watanabe's deft skill at creating sculptural forms that stimulate the viewer, and of his free abandon at cladding commonplace apartments with a futurist facade. In addition, the stepped or sawtooth plan of the New Sky Building No. 3 affords each room a southern exposure on a fairly narrow lot.

Some architects equate the futurist imagery of Watanabe with the visionary sketches of Eric Mendelsohn,[44] but it should be remembered that Mendelsohn's most dynamic designs generally occurred before 1930, when the entire modern movement was fascinated with the potential of the machine aesthetic. Today, Watanabe's designs are enjoyable to look at, but seem to be something of an anachronism.

Everyman Architecture: The Industrialization of Bourgeois Japan

The final chapter on industrialized building isn't being written in the university laboratories nor in the sophisticated arena of mixed-systems architecture. It is being written in the hamburger drive-ins, in the outdoor recreation tents, and in the floating playgrounds of fun architecture. This is the test of industrialization; whether it can stand up to the use and abuse of the average citizen. Thus far, all indications are that architechnology is diverse and elastic enough to serve almost any need.

One of the leading protagonists of this movement is the Ogawa® Tent Company. Founded in 1914, the company has a long history of manufacturing practical, everyday goods, including such diverse items as awnings, tents, rafts, fishery tools, rainproof goods, and prefabricated provisional structures. The Ogawa® Tent Company manufactured no less than eight different pneumatic structures at Expo '70, including the remarkable Fuji Group Pavil-

161

162

163

164

160.
Yamazaki House No. 2, Yoji Watanabe, 1973: An urban residence conceived as a mini-capsule tower in silver, finally built in concrete and painted black. Each room resembles a Pullman railroad car in its long, narrow proportions.
161.
Geodesic Drive-In, Oiso Long Beach: Techno-hamburgers in a mega-amusement park. (See figure 324.)
162.
Airpoline®, Ogawa® Tent Company: An inflatable playhouse.
163, 164.
Daika Dream House: A space capsule for play equally at home, on land or sea.

ion designed by Yutaka Murata. Their latest creation is the Airpoline®, a 21-ft (6.4-m) diameter, 12-ft (3.7-m) high, multi-purpose, pneumatic tent. With or without its dome-shaped roof, the Airpoline® can serve as a children's playroom, holding 15 comfortably, or as additional living space to be attached anywhere onto an existing residence. Available in a rainbow of colors, the canvas-and-clear-plastic structure comes complete with two pneumatic air pumps for about $7,500.00. Besides manufacturing this minibuilding, the Ogawa® Tent Company is continuing to employ their considerable pneumatic structure expertise to cover swimming pools, ice-skating rinks and bowling alleys. They have also developed a wide variety of stretched canvas awnings to cover golf driving ranges, snack bars, and many of the common facilities normally considered taboo by "serious" architects.

The indefatigable Kisho Kurokawa has also applied his technological know-how to the design of everyman architecture. At the Odakyu Drive-in in Otome, Kurokawa utilized a steel-pipe space frame to support a capsule restaurant. Furthermore, the tent structure on the roof serves as an open-air beer garden. A short drive from Kurokawa's space-frame drive-in is the Oiso Long Beach poolside restaurant—a bright orange geodesic dome, serving up such twentieth-century delights as an instant microwave cheeseburger. When Bucky Fuller's genius filters down to the ubiquitous hamburger joint, you know architechnology is here to stay.

Even the once-independent world of marine architecture cannot escape the ripples of the wave. The floating Daika Dream House is nothing short of a space capsule on water. The FRP structure is finished to endure wind and rain and is guaranteed not to deteriorate under normal use. The Daika Dream House comes equipped with carpeted floors, mattress, ventilation unit, and electrical receptacles for the optional electric generator. The over-all height is 8 ft 4 in (2.5 m) and the over-all width is 13 ft 8 in (4 m). The unit can house a family of five comfortably, and sells in Japan for about $3,000. It is touted by its manufacturer to be perfect as a summer lake house, a beach house, a camping retreat, tea house, or ski house. Whatever its application, it is obvious even to the most casual observer that the country with the fastest-growing Gross National Product in the world is applying industrial technology to everything that floats, rolls or stands still.

In many respects Japan is the testing ground for the superindustrial, densely packed, techno-society toward which the urbanizing world is moving. Whether we will be able to adapt our built environments to the ever-changing demands of such a society is a question architects the world over are grappling with. In order to answer this question we must analyze the most advanced, outer reaches of existing society. We must study the developments in architechnology, be they plug-in capsules, inflatable restaurants, or floating playhouses. Surely if we can "learn from Las Vegas," then maybe we can also "benefit from Benihana."

165.
Odakyu Drive-In, Otome, Kisho Kurokawa, 1969: A space-frame drive-in restaurant with a tensile-structure beer garden under a tent roof. The ubiquitous Mr. Kurokawa has applied his skill and imagination to the fast-food world of everyman architecture.

4.
Form and Space: Several Interpretations

Many observers of Japan's architecture have concluded that the Japanese revere form and ignore space. Kenzo Tange himself has explained that there is no traditional piazza in Japanese towns and therefore no concept of urban space in the Western sense. The entire Renaissance affair with space, beginning with the discovery of perspective and evolving into what Bruno Zevi labeled, "Architecture as Space,"[45] seems to never have entered the minds of the Japanese. In 1427 Masaccio completed his painting of The Holy Trinity, drawing great attention to the use of perspective to define and articulate space. Wylie Sypher explained how, "The walls of the enclosing painted 'chapel' recede with mathematical precision toward a vanishing point indicated by the feet of Christ in the foreground plane."[46]

While the use of perspective was being refined during the quattrocento by Renaissance masters like Masaccio and Raphael, as in his School of Athens (1509–1511), on the other side of the globe their equally masterful contemporary, Sesshū (1420–1506), was celebrating the insignificance of man in relation to nature. His exquisite scroll of the four seasons, painted in 1486, was the epitome of Muromachi ink painting in which Sesshū "tended to flatten out the space and emphasize strong linear patterns."[47] Ignoring whatever inkling he may have had about how mathematical geometrics might have rendered greater depth and realism in his art, Sesshū focused on the implication of space through flattened planes and broken, unfinished lines—a concept in painting later deified in the West as cubism. Notwithstanding the effects that Japanese wood-block prints had on European artists in the nineteenth century, it is doubtful that Sesshū himself ever influenced the work of Cezanne, Picasso, or Braque. Still, it is edifying to realize that the techniques

and traditions used to modulate and define space throughout the 2,600 years of Japanese civilization were deeply rooted and evolved within very restrictive guidelines; what might at first glance seem to be lines randomly placed in a flat field, may in fact be solids and planes carefully placed in very deep, if not infinite space.

Just as the relation of objects in space plays an important role in understanding Sesshū's paintings, the interplay of solids within a void plays a key role in understanding the evolution of Japanese architecture. Fumihiko Maki has explained that the principle governing the design of the seventh-century masterpiece, Horyuji Temple, is one of Compositional Form[48] in which various objects are arranged within a frame. This concept no doubt originated in China, but was borrowed by Japan directly from Korea. Although it is common for each object to be treated separately by

166.
Gunma Prefectural Museum of Fine Art, Arata Isozaki, 1974. (See figures 259–264.)

art historians examining the *Pagoda* or the *Kondo* alone, it is the sequence of spaces experienced as one approaches and enters the *Chumon,* or Middle Gate and then moves through the central court towards the lecture hall that truly reveals the composition of the carefully hewn wooden structures as they relate to each other. The concept of sequential spaces in architecture and of layering flattened planes in painting are by now familiar to most students of traditional Japanese culture. Of equal importance, however, is the fact that these concepts did not originate in Japan, but were borrowed from her neighbors, Korea and China, then assimilated, refined, and eventually made an integral part of the concepts that dominated her artistic growth for more than a thousand years.

From this brief discussion of Japanese art, three important points emerge: first, that the very concept of space and how one shapes it has a history in the East different from that of the West; second, that the changes and developments made in Japanese art over a thousand-year period were dominated if not controlled by unwritten laws which allowed only the slightest deviation from the past; and, third, that as an island nation Japan was wont to borrow aspects of foreign cultures and then recede into her isolation, and alter, transform, and evolve that borrowed culture to fit her own situation. These three points play a key role in the conceptualization and development of space in architecture on that island.

167.
The Holy Trinity, Masaccio, 1427: The powerful use of one-point perspective gave great depth to the architectonic paintings of this Renaissance master.
168.
Winter Landscape, Sesshū, 1486: One segment of his timeless scroll of the four seasons, this ink painting employs broken lines and flattened planes to imply space, rather than define it with the mathematical precision of his Western counterparts.

The transition from feudal farmers to industrial giants, from warmakers to peace-lovers, from Geisha houses to Playboy® Clubs has also had a profound effect on this small nation; yet she has absorbed alien elements as she has always done, she has digested them, and to the amazement, amusement, and sometimes horror of the Occidental, has made them an integral part of what is today Japan. For the young architect learning his profession in postwar Japan, the tensions between traditional patterns and new, Western concepts must have been excruciating. From wood and paper, one learned steel and concrete; from subtle and restrained, one learned bold and brutal; from centuries of meditating on the implications of Sesshū, one undertook to master an alien alphabet, a distant art history, and a strange architectural evolution that included such diverse luminaries as Michelangelo, Borromini, Balthazar Neumann, and eventually Wright, Corbu, Mies, and Gropius. With the humility of the vanquished and the industriousness of the indefatigable,

168

the Japanese architect began his apprenticeship. He studied and traveled. He learned English, French, and German. He enrolled at Harvard, Yale, and Columbia; and he worked for LeCorbusier, Wright, and Gropius. Eventually he returned home and tried to relate a 2,500-year-old tradition to a 25-year-old, freshly borrowed culture.

Different men have predictably responded in different ways to this dilemma. Some have sought and found methods of reproducing traditional Japanese architectural elements in new materials. Others have evolved a modern vocabulary subtly reflecting Oriental forms and spaces. And still others have rejected the past, and embraced the present and future with enormous energy and creativity.

Following is the work of several prominent architects, each of whom has resolved the dilemma in his own way. Included in this chapter is the architecture of Kimio Yokoyama, Fumihiko Maki, Arata Isozaki, Minoru Takeyama, and Shin'ichi Okada.

169, 170.
Horyuji Temple, Nara, Seventh Century: This ancient temple epitomizes the traditional Japanese concept of Compositional Form, in which objects are placed within a frame. The frame is punctured on the left by the *chumon*, or Middle Gate, and is accented on the right by the large lecture hall. The pagoda and *kondo*, or Goldon Hall, are arranged above and below the central axis.

171.
Toshogu Shrine, Nikko, Seventeenth Century: This elaborate mausoleum represents the zenith in Japanese ornate detailing and baroque forms. (See figure 1.)

172.
Himeji Castle, completed 1624: Considered the finest and best-preserved of the fortified castles built throughout Japan during the seventeenth century. The series of labyrinthine walls and moats were copied from Western fortifications after the introduction of firearms.

170

173

174

175

176

173–175.
Yamanashi Communications Center, Kenzo Tange &
URTEC, 1966: The closest Tange ever came to
realizing his proposed megastructure, the vertical core
shafts and interlocking bridge elements symbolized
the Metabolist movement. (See figure 37.)

176.
Tochigi Prefectural Conference Hall, Masato Otaka,
1970: The interlocking precast concrete framework
evokes the post-and-beam aesthetic of Japanese
temple architecture. (See figures 65, 66.)

177.
Kyoto International Conference Hall, Sachio Otani,
1966: Like a massive ship in dry dock, this
competition-winning precast concrete scheme is
reminiscent of the ancestral wood structures, first
used to build Japan's Shinto Shrines two thousand
years ago. (See figures 77, 78.)

178.
Kibogaoka Youth Castle, Tatsuhiko Nakajima & GAUS,
1972: This assemblage of architechnology mixes
conventional construction with the best in clip-on
capsules and plug-in modules. (See figures 97, 149–
154.)

177

179

180

179, 180.
Tsukuba University, Fumihiko Maki, 1974: The taut, glass block facade stretched across the rectangular frame achieves what Maki calls "a small, glassy mountain" as the focus of the university new town. (See figures 215–220.)

181, 182.
National Aquarium, Fumihiko Maki, 1975: On-site prefabrication of concrete arches simplified the erection process. Their juxtaposition provides a successful interplay of solid and void, and light and shade. (See figures 227–233.)

183.
Oita Medical Hall, Arata Isozaki, 1960 and 1972: Bold forms and heavy massing characterize Isozaki's early sculptural designs. (See figures 242–248.)

184.
Fukuoka Sogo Bank, Headquarters, Arata Isozaki, 1972: The interpenetration of forms set against the large red wall heightens the tension in this innovative and inspired building. (See figures 249–258.)

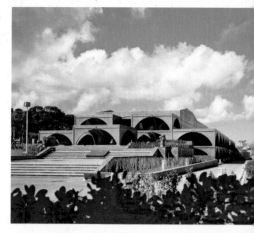
181

182

183

184

185

186

187

185.
Nibankan, Minoru Takeyama, 1970: The symbol of post-Modern architecture as defined by Charles Jencks, this mixture of supergraphics and catalogue components is a testimony to Takeyama's skill at being able to make a significant statement out of a collection of discarded and fragmented parts. (See figure 270.)
186.
Korakuen Yellow Building, Takenaka Construction Company, 1973: An urban pleasure palace and recreation center. (See figures 325–327.)
187.
Pepsi-Cola® Canning Plant, Minoru Takeyama, 1972: Geometric forms combined with high-tech imagery dominate Takeyama's resourceful architectural design. (See figure 272.)

188.
New Sky Building No. 3, Yoji Watanabe, 1967: Conceived as a wall of silver Airstream® mobile homes, this facade of technology is strengthened by its use of the machine aesthetic. (See figure 157.)
189.
Zooming Lights, Shinjuku, Tokyo, 1974: Japan races toward the future as the electrographic architecture of its urban centers symbolizes its technological growth, its self-confidence and creative artistry.

190.
Sho-Hondo, Kimio Yokoyama, 1972: At the base of Mt.
Fuji, this imposing structure is the main sanctuary and
symbolic heart of the Sokagakkai, a sect of Buddhism
claiming a following of nearly eight million families.
191.
Main Gate, Sho-Hondo: The post-tension, precast
concrete elements imitate the traditional temple gate.

190

Kimio Yokoyama: Devotion to a Religious Order

Kimio Yokoyama was born in Chiba, outside Tokyo, in 1924. He studied architecture at Yasuda Industrial School at Waseda University, receiving his degree in 1948. In 1955 he established his own office and for the last two decades has devoted his practice almost solely to the religious architecture of the Sokagakkai (literally: Value-Creating Academic Society). The Sokagakkai is the association of lay adherents of Nichiren Shoshu, one of the many Nichiren sects of Buddhism.

Nichiren Shoshu is said to have maintained itself through 66 generations of high priests. The Sokagakkai, however, was formed in 1930 by Tsunesaburo Makiguchi, who was imprisoned during World War II for not worshipping the Sun Goddess. Makiguchi died in prison, but his closest follower, Josei Toda, was released in July, 1945. Toda devoted his final years to an intensive proselytizing campaign.

His pleas for self-improvement were warmly received in postwar Japan, and by 1957 Sokagakkai claimed 750,000 families. In recent years, membership has mushroomed to a world population of 7,570,000 families (according to Sokagakkai figures released October 16, 1972). In order to serve these swelling numbers, Kimio Yokoyama designed a structure consuming ten million man-hours and requiring $120 million to complete. (One Dollar = 300 Yen.)

192.
Sho-Hondo: The heavy-handed juxtaposition of
disparate, monumental forms further weakens this
ostentatious project.

192

193

194

193–195.
Sho-Hondo: These photographs trace the spatial sequence from the Garden of the Law, the plaza facing the Pavilion of Perfect Harmony (193), through the Temple of Purification (194) into the Mystic Sanctuary (195), which is in itself an impressive, but architecturally unresolved space.

It is a sprawling complex organized around a linear spine. Influenced by traditional Japanese religious architecture, Yokoyama attempted to create a sequence of spaces beginning with a General Gate moving up to a Temple Gate and eventually arriving at the *Sho-Hondo,* or Temple itself. The Temple has been further divided into a sequence of spaces leading the worshipper from a gathering space, through a transition space, to a lobby space, and finally to the sanctuary. These areas have been given pompous names in keeping with the ostentatious monumentality of the entire project. The gathering

space or plaza is called "The Garden of the Law"; the transition space is called "The Pavilion of Perfect Harmony"; the entrance lobby is called "The Temple of Purification"; and the sanctuary is called "The Mystic Sanctuary."

With the greatest of intentions and with considerable resources, both financial and spiritual, Yokoyama created an enormous disappointment. While employing the traditional Japanese concept of sequential spaces, he failed to include any of the subtleties that bring about the fascination and intrigue of the ancient Temples of

Japan. One searches in vain for the framed view of the minor focus, or for the series of glimpses of a piece of architecture from various angles and elevations as one builds toward a crescendo. None of the elements of surprise, of wit, or of humility are exhibited in this massive overdose of flamboyant materials and conflicting forms all screaming for recognition.

Accepting that the Sho-Hondo is in the garish school of religious architecture, one is apt to conclude that it is perhaps based on the precedent of the Toshogu Mausoleum at Nikko, which is rich in gold

195

leaf, and itself flamboyant in form. However, unlike Nikko, the Sho-Hondo is not held together by one architectural vocabulary, but is rather several disparate dialects all arguing amongst themselves, with no single statement being clearly communicated.

Some critics of the Sho-Hondo have said that the unbroken linear approach down endless paths and winding ramps gives people, "the sense of being transported on conveyor belts." While I must agree that the sensation of being herded toward

some massive collection point is experienced, it must be said that upon finally entering the sanctuary there is a certain magnificence of scale and grandeur that almost makes it all worthwhile, though not quite. The semirigid suspension-structure roof, resembling a spoked wheel, is supported by massive fan-shaped buttresses straining in every direction. The structure has been hailed as an engineering wonder of the twentieth century, affording 600 priests and 5,400 worshippers an unobstructed view of the Dai-Gohonzon, or Holy Scriptures. As the visitor plods his

way past pavilions of perfect harmony and temples of purification, he is reminded by contrast of the simplicity of Kenzo Tange's 1964 Olympic Stadium or of the delicate lightness of Bucky Fuller's domes that have inspired newer domes covering fifty, sixty and now seventy thousand spectators, each with an unobstructed view of his most highly worshipped god or goddess; and he cannot avoid wondering if all the Moroccan marble, Italian marble, sulfurized bronze and chipped granite might have been unnecessary.

196

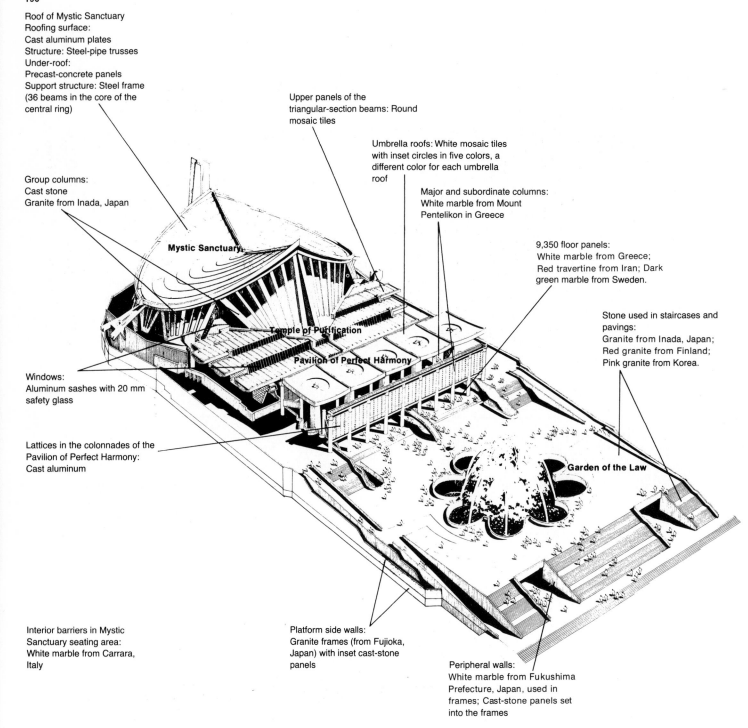

Roof of Mystic Sanctuary
Roofing surface:
Cast aluminum plates
Structure: Steel-pipe trusses
Under-roof:
Precast-concrete panels
Support structure: Steel frame
(36 beams in the core of the
central ring)

Upper panels of the
triangular-section beams: Round
mosaic tiles

Umbrella roofs: White mosaic tiles
with inset circles in five colors, a
different color for each umbrella
roof

Major and subordinate columns:
White marble from Mount
Pentelikon in Greece

Group columns:
Cast stone
Granite from Inada, Japan

9,350 floor panels:
White marble from Greece;
Red travertine from Iran; Dark
green marble from Sweden.

Stone used in staircases and
pavings:
Granite from Inada, Japan;
Red granite from Finland;
Pink granite from Korea.

Mystic Sanctuary

Temple of Purification

Pavilion of Perfect Harmony

Windows:
Aluminum sashes with 20 mm
safety glass

Lattices in the colonnades of the
Pavilion of Perfect Harmony:
Cast aluminum

Garden of the Law

Interior barriers in Mystic
Sanctuary seating area:
White marble from Carrara,
Italy

Platform side walls:
Granite frames (from Fujioka,
Japan) with inset cast-stone
panels

Peripheral walls:
White marble from Fukushima
Prefecture, Japan, used in
frames; Cast-stone panels set
into the frames

110

197

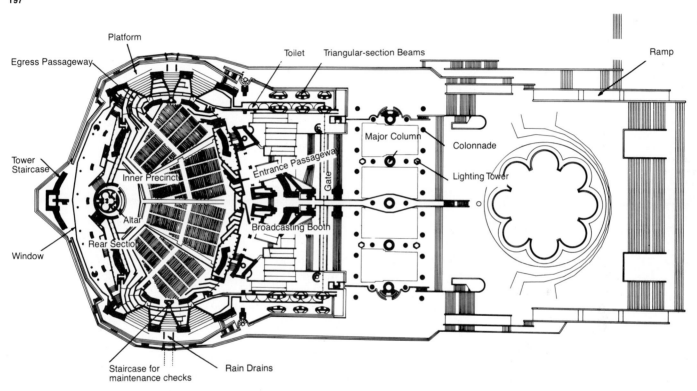

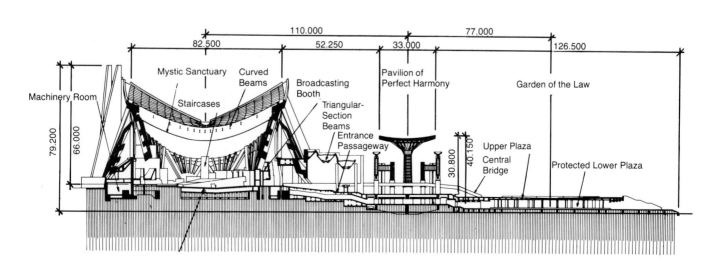

198.
Kato Gakuen Elementary School, Fumihiko Maki,
1972: In this "school like a large house," Maki employs
a pattern of interior courtyards which spatially
separate the "rooms" of the house but allow visual
connections. The building is unified by a consistent
architectural vocabulary which metaphorically evokes
the image of an ocean liner.

Fumihiko Maki: Contextualism, Physical and Cultural

The diversity of Fumihiko Maki's architecture does not project a particular style or visual trademark, yet it is bound together by a strong adherence to a design philosophy. An early indication of this philosophy can be found in an article that Maki coauthored with Masato Otaka in the spring of 1960, in which he states:

"There is no more critically concerned observer of our rapidly changing society than the urban designer. Charged with

giving form—with perceiving and contributing order—to agglomerates of buildings, highways, and greenspaces in which men have increasingly come to work and live, the urban designer stands between technology and human need and seeks to make the first a servant, for the second must be paramount in a civilized world."[49]

Several key thoughts present themselves. First, that as an architect, Maki perceives the need to contribute order. Secondly, he is aware of design through the eyes of an urbanist. Thirdly, he must make technology a servant of human need.

Although he is one of the original Metabolist Group, Maki perceives the group to have been more of a collection of contemporaries than a cohesive movement, and by his own admission, stands outside the philosophy that has come to be associated with the Metabolists. In 1964 he published a small book at Washington University, St. Louis, as an Associate Professor, entitled, *Investigations in Collective Form*. In it he advocated the value of collective form as an approach to architectural design, versus the accepted theory of architecture as single buildings.

The whole tenor and import of his early writing and research involved perceiving the environment from the point of view of an urban designer in which each element was part of a larger whole. Even today he confesses that among his favorite aphorisms is Aldo Van Eyck's "A city is like a house and a house like a small city." This attitude that, "each part is a small realized whole" and that, "the composite whole is suggested by its parts," is basic to Maki's design philosophy.

His work tends to be more individually responsive to environmental pressures

199

199–202.
Interiors, Kato Gakuen Elementary School: The skilled manipulation of space, the quality of light, the use of Ray Komai's fun graphics, and the functional organization give this school a charm and excitement that make the architecture part of the educational experience.

203.
Site Plan, Kato Gakuen Elementary School.

204.
Axonometric, Kato Gakuen Elementary School: The interpenetration of voids within the mass of the building creates what Maki calls "thick transparent walls" between the classrooms.

and context[50], both physical and cultural, and less concerned with creating technologically advanced panaceas for large urban areas. You will find no plug-in capsules or service towers connected by bridges in the sky among Maki's urbane solutions. He employs technology as a tool to serve man, rather than seeking solutions through technology itself. He believes the dreams of the First Machine Age and the Metabolist movement cannot be fulfilled, and that it is unrealistic to try. He is fond of quoting Reyner Banham who said, "It may well be that what we have hitherto understood as architecture, and

199

200

201

202

what we are beginning to understand of technology are incompatible disciplines.''[51]

Maki is a traditional architect in that he is concerned with fulfilling the requirements of the program, in relating the building to its surroundings, and in achieving what Bruno Zevi called, ''Architecture as Space.''[52] More than any other single theme, Maki's work is bound together by an unending search to modulate, shape and develop spaces that serve and stimulate the inhabitants of his structures. His early Golgi Structures were an anti-Meta-bolist system of spaces shaping solids, rather than machines shaping spaces. His plan for the Rissho University campus is held together by a system of interlocking plazas articulated by shifts in axis, changes in level, and a layering of transparent surfaces. His recent work exhibits a continued interest in defining space, in developing construction technology to serve specific projects, and in creating an architecture that gives people a unique sense of place.

School Like a Large House
In the Kato Gakuen elementary school,

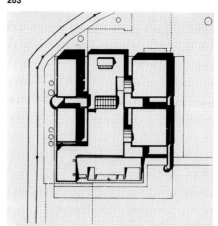

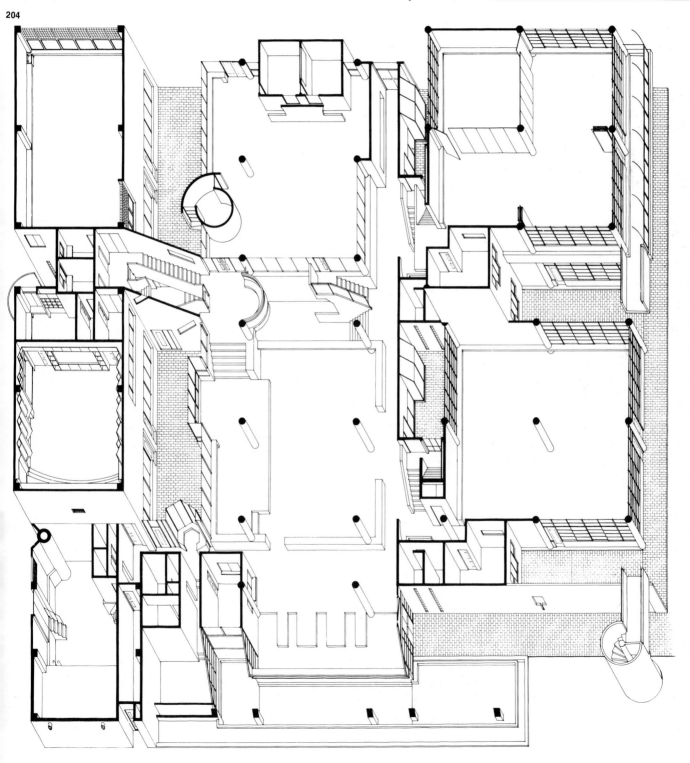

completed in 1972, Maki was faced with designing the first open-plan school in Japan. The need for students to relate to each other without the needless intrusion of outside noise was solved by separating the classrooms with seven interior courtyards, which Maki prefers to call "thick, transparent walls." These oblong courtyards bring the separate spaces together much in the manner of a large house, giving the individual rooms a sense of the whole, while increasing the legibility of the spaces themselves. Identity and surprise are rendered throughout the school by the use of supergraphics designed by Ray Komai.

From the exterior, the school is a restrained exercise in simplicity and diminutive scale in deference to the children who use it. Maki explains that he prefers work "that quietly receives entrants." Generally his architecture is characterized by a nonmonumental approach which suggests rather than reveals the interior's dramatic spatial development.

On-Site Prefabrication
The site of the Osaka Prefectural Sports Center posed a more difficult problem. Located at the edge of a traditional, low-scale residential neighborhood, the sports

center faces across a canal toward a large, industrial complex. The curved steel surfaces reflect the gently sloping, tiled roofs of the residential quarter, while gradually stepping up from one story on the residential side, to a bold silhouette facing the industrial complex.

Within the building, Maki unifies the separate spaces with a central spine. Reminiscent of a narrow urban street, this linear space expands and contracts, stepping down to the gymnasium and up to a framed view of the industrial complex and a second-level observation-deck restau-

205

206

207

rant. The visitor is reminded of the miniature *pensions* of Venice overlooking a busy piazza, or of the intimate *kissaten* (second-story coffee shops) set above dense urban streets throughout Japan.

From the restaurant, Maki evolves a layering of spaces through a series of transparent surfaces. One can dine in peaceful quiet looking back through the central space over a roof garden, to the entrance plaza below. This interest in layering transparent planes and spaces is manifest in much of Maki's work. From the student center at Rissho University to the mini-

shops at the Hillside Terrace Apartments, the visitor is treated to an articulated view through a communication space back toward a busy, colorful gathering place. At Rissho it is the main campus plaza; at the Hillside Apartments it is a silent movie of taxis, cars, and pedestrian bridges over a major intersection. This layering effect lends definition to the spaces while offering the visitor, in a subtle way, a visual reminder of the landscape he has just passed through, without the sensory overload of taxi horns and traffic noise.

One of the outstanding features of the Osaka Sports Center, completed in 1972, is its method of construction. Confronted with a confined space, Maki and his associates devised a system of prefabricated roof units, which were factory produced to the maximum lengths allowed by transportation codes. In an area adjacent to the site, thse units were then fitted with roofing plates, interior insulation, HVAC ducts and equipment, light fixture stabilizers, and the finished ceiling mesh. The roof units, each weighing several tons, were lifted into place by cranes and bolted to long-span, cylindrical steel beams. Con-

208

205–207.
Osaka Prefectural Sports Center, Fumihiko Maki, 1972: This linear building steps up from its residential neighbors on the east to the heavy industrial surroundings on the west. Major sports facilities, including the gymnasium (206) and the swimming pool, are organized along a central spine (207).
208, 209.
Structure, Osaka Prefectural Sports Center: The on-site prefabrication of curved, steel-trussed roof panels (208) allowed for simple and quick erection on a tight site. Roof members are suspended from large steel roof beams (209), creating major column-free spaces for spectator sports.

209

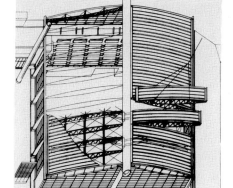

struction of the entire superstructure took place in only 16 days. In recent years, Maki and Associates has continued to experiment with on-site prefabrication, both at Tsukuba University and at the National Aquarium at Expo '75 in Okinawa.

An Aggregate of Urban Places
The Hillside Terrace Apartments, located in Daikanyama, Tokyo, form an incremental urban housing system set along a busy city street. Phase two was opened in 1973, and Phase three in 1976, completing the final section of an extended hierarchy of public, semipublic, and semiprivate spaces. Parallel to the axis of the street, Maki achieves a succession of different volumes by slight changes in level and by an eroding of the solid mass into a series of linked open and semiopen spaces. Rather than setting the apartments on *pilotis*,[53] Maki brings the solid surface to the ground, giving the visitor a sense of enclosure, while simultaneously opening selected sections of the solid to allow what Maki calls a "penetration of the landscape." This system of framed vistas and double transparency integrates the interior and exterior spaces. By opening the plaza in Phase two towards an ancient

211

212

213

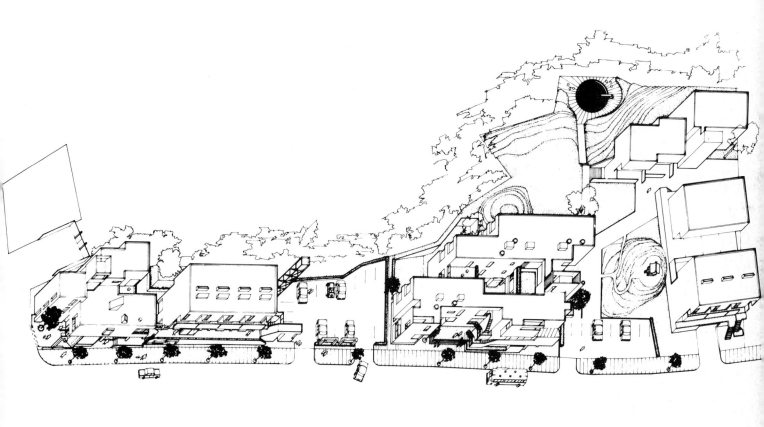

210–214.
Hillside Terrace Apartments, Fumihiko Maki, 1976:
Parallel to a major street, Maki created a hierarchy of
public, semi-public, and private urban places. Through
the use of glass and implied vertical planes, layering of
transparent and semi-transparent volumes provides
contextual connections to the urban surroundings, but
allows a distinct identity for the residential plazas.

214

park on the south, Maki retains elements of the landscape that existed years before, while introducing glimpses of the urban street to the north, creating a continuity of space and time. Maki has said that, "urban design is an aggregate of small-scale places." The variety and surprise condensed into the Hillside Terrace Apartments provide an aggregate of human-scale places that are both functional and fun.

A Small, Glassy Mountain
At the foot of Mount Tsukuba (rhymes with scuba) in Ibaraki Prefecture, about 60 miles north of Tokyo, the Japan Housing Corporation has begun development of a Research and Education Newtown. Scheduled to house some 130,000 academicians and related personnel, it is a vigorous attempt to shift population growth away from Japan's big cities. In his book, Nihon Retto Kaizoron (*Building a New Japan: A Plan for Remodeling the Japanese Archipelago*[54]), former Prime Minister, Kakuei Tanaka, called for the decentralization of Japanese universities and industrial complexes. While in office he claimed that Tsukuba Newtown would help alleviate Tokyo's congestion and create an ideal academic environment.

The focus of the Newtown is Tsukuba University, the first phase of which includes the central building (art studios, classrooms and research laboratories), the library, cafeteria, and gymnasium. Maki and Associates was commissioned to design the central building and the library, completed in 1974.

The central building straddles the main north-south axis which forms the central spine of the master plan, acting as a gateway to the heart of the campus. Built on a flat plateau, the symbolic seven-story gateway reads, according to Maki, as "a

215

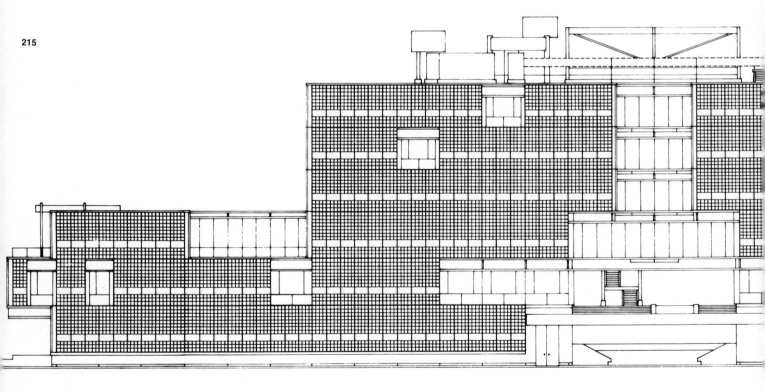

small, glassy mountain'' against the towering Mount Tsukuba beyond.

The central building itself runs along an east-west axis and is divided into three zones; the art department and physical education department at either end, with the communal zone in the center. The intersection of the building's east-west axis with the main campus' north-south spine is developed into a large ''city-room'' first conceived by Maki in the early sixties and executed on a more diminutive scale at the Senri Town Center outside Osaka. The seven-story space links the two major

215.
Tsukuba University, Central Building, South Elevation, Fumihiko Maki, 1974: At the time this building was completed, Maki declared, ''The age of the great experiments has ended, and the architect must try to find his own sense of reality.'' In his own attempts to take his architecture beyond Metabolism and the radical proposals of the 60s, Maki has further developed his interest in ''surface membrane'' enclosures, in layers of transparency and in shaping space to a degree of refinement and elegance which marks a new direction for Japanese architecture. (See color plates 179, 180.)

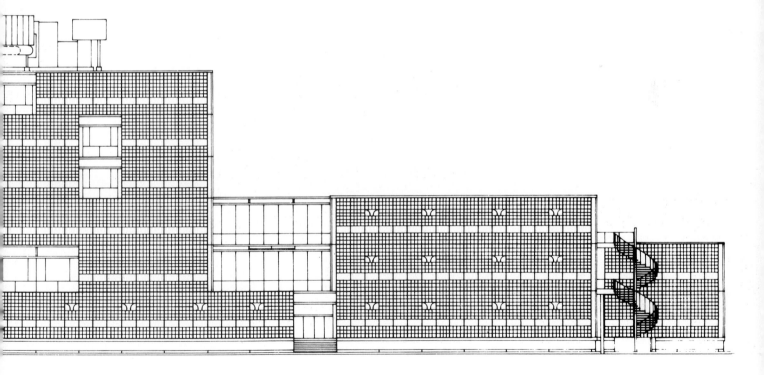

functional clusters with the student lounge, lockers, cafeteria, and various informal gathering places.

The most arresting feature of the building is its glass block-enclosure. The $5 million facility had to enclose 200,000 sq ft (18,600 m²) at the low cost of $25/sq ft with a very tight construction schedule. To meet these constraints Maki and Associates developed a system of dry construction (no poured concrete and no masonry). Interior partitions are of cast-aluminum panels and lightweight steel studs, floors are skeleton-steel deck plates, and the curtain wall is primarily 8-in × 8-in (20-cm × 20-cm) amber glass blocks fitted inside 5-ft × 12-ft (1.2-m × 3.7-m) steel frames. The on-site assembly of steel-framed blocks created large panels which were then hoisted in place by cranes.

Students of architectural history will undoubtedly recognize the influence of Pierre Chareau's Maison de Verre, 1932, which Maki visited at the insistence of his friend Aldo Van Eyck. Like Maison de Verre, which Kenneth Frampton explained "is inherently organized as a series of vertical planes or layers of space preceeding frontally from the forecourt,"[55] the Central Building at Tsukuba is organized as a set of layered spaces. The glass block's transparency is phenomenal rather than literal; however, it does create good sound and weather insulation while showering the classrooms with natural light. The translucent panels are punctuated by clear panels, offering framed views from the classrooms and a large unobstructed panorama from the central, communal space.

Motor Museum
A less industrial-looking and far more personal statement by Maki and Associates

219

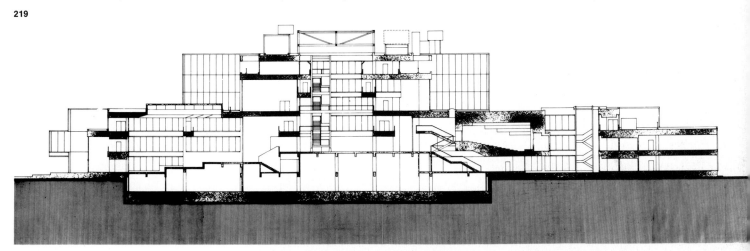

216–218.
Tsukuba University, Central Building: On-site prefab of large panels of glass block (218) create the skin of the building (216) which encloses, but is distinct from, the major internal spaces (217).

219, 220.
Section and Site Plan, Tsukuba University, Central Building:

1. Indoor Swimming Pool
2. Central Building
3. Art Department
4. Physical Education Dept.
5. Design Dept.
6. Library
7. Gymnasium I
8. Cafeteria
9. Gymnasium II
10. Pedestrian Deck
11. Sunken Garden
12. Access Road

220

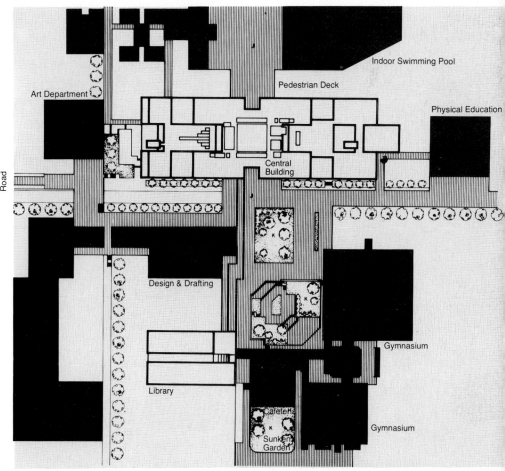

was completed in the same year for the Toyota® Motor Company. It is the Toyota Kuragaike Commemorative Hall. The structure is set against the magnificent scenery of Kuragaike Lake. As one approaches the site from the city of Toyota (where else?) the scenic beauty dominates the landscape, while the low profile of the building modestly comes into view. The building is functionally divided into two separate and distinct zones; a guest house for visiting VIP's, and a public museum and exhibition hall. Maki wisely set the public area partially below ground level, allowing the natural setting to dominate the landscape.

The two distinctly different functions of the building are set within two bold geometric triangles loosely connected by a central spine. Within the triangles, Maki carefully frames views of private gardens and the distant lake with the same dexterity and skill that is apparent in his previous work. The prominent geometric forms, however, seem inappropriate and willful in the natural setting.

Inside the elegantly appointed guest house, Maki has introduced curved, stepped, coffered ceilings which present a playful relief from the hard geometry. Maki claims that perhaps he is "getting baroque." In actual fact, the deft integration of hard geometry with gentle curves is prevalent in Maki's work from the early Mogusa Town Center to the Osaka Sports Center and is probably most successful at the Expo '75 Aquarium in Okinawa. At the Toyota Commemorative Hall, however, one senses that the geometric interlocking triangles are less successful than the restrained simplicity of Maki's other projects.

221

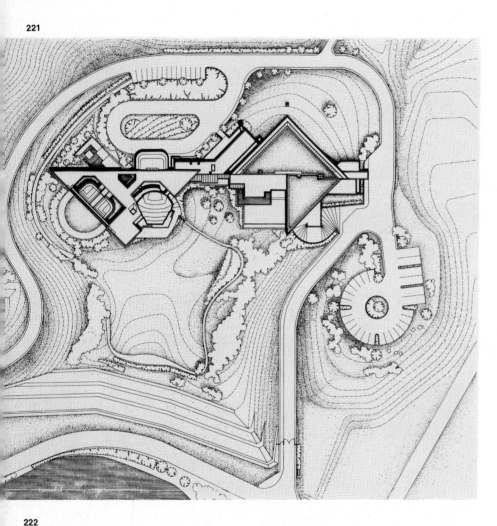

222

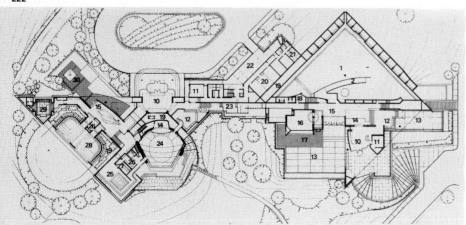

223

221–223.
Toyota Kuragaike Commemorative Hall, Fumihiko Maki, 1974: Willful and baroque, the bold geometrics, connected by a central spine, fit tenuously into their lush natural setting.

1. Exhibition Hall	16. Ishida Room
2. Ramp	17. Pond
3. Sub-Entrance	18. Projection Room
4. Lounge	19. Court
5. Storage Area	20. Anteroom
6. Control Room	21. Guard Room
7. Machine Room	22. Service Yard
8. Kitchen	23. Corridor (spine)
9. Dressing Room	24. Reception Room
10. Entrance Hall	25. Dining Room
11. Office	26. Bar
12. Lounge	27. Pantry
13. Terrace	28. VIP Reception Room
14. Stage	29. Japanese Room
15. Lobby	30. Fountain

224.
Mogusa Town Center, Fumihiko Maki, 1969: The free-form objects in counterpoint to the hard rectangular frame are an early indication of Maki's interest in dynamic spatial relationships.
225, 226.
Interiors, Toyota Kuragaike Commemorative Hall: Curvilinear, coffered ceiling forms and framed views help create distinct, interesting interior spaces.

Slices of the Sea

On July 20, 1975, the much-heralded International Ocean Exposition opened on the Motobu Penninsula at the northern end of Okinawa, for a period of six months. The theme of Expo '75 was "The Sea We Want to See," and no building fulfills the theme better than the National Aquarium by Fumihiko Maki and Associates. It is the principal building in the Fish Cluster, one of four clusters of pavilions demonstrating man's relation to the ocean. The other three clusters highlight the following: People and History, Science and Technology, and Ships. Other exhibits include a

224

226

floating city called Aquapolis by Kiyonori Kikutake, a marine park, a beach, a seaside bazaar, an administration center, and transportation facilities.

The Marine Life Park consists of the aquarium proper, the dolphin island, a plaza, and a green area. It is scheduled to become a permanent national facility. Unlike its predecessors around the globe, the Okinawa Aquarium does not use isolated little windows like the outside of an airplane to view the high-pressure fluid world within, but employs high-strength plastic tanks to create vast "slices of the sea" completely visible to the large crowds. One tank illustrates the coral sea and features schools of rainbow-colored tropical fish, while the other shows a glimpse of the outer ocean and its myriad of inhabitants.

Due to the subtropical climate of Okinawa, Maki thoughtfully created a path of shade linking the waiting lines of visitors with the Cluster Plaza. This path of shade is formed by an arcade of on-site, prefabricated, quarter circles intersecting at 90°. Poured adjacent to the construction site itself, the reinforced-concrete components contain self-forming joints for ease of erection. This intelligent application of technology eliminated the need for transporting heavy structural members from the main islands of Japan. The result is a successful interplay of solid and void with continually shifting patterns of light and shade. One is reminded of the simple arches of Louis Kahn's Indian Institute of

227

Management in Ahmedabad, and his Capital complex in Dacca, Bangladesh.

In the National Aquarium at Expo '75, Maki achieves functional variety and spatial interest employing a straightforward, modest architectural language. This is his forte—to transform a complex program into a legible set of spaces with a simple enclosure that appears reserved at first glance, but with continued investigation reveals dramatic spatial development, wit, and human scale.

227.
National Aquarium, Fumihiko Maki, 1975: The focus of the Marine Life Park developed for Expo '75 in Okinawa. The "path of shade" provided by the arched colonnade is reminiscent of Louis Kahn's work in India and Bangladesh. (See color plates 181, 182.)

Looking back to the visions of the Metabolist group, Maki explains that, ''the age of the great experiments has ended, and the architect must try to find his own sense of reality.'' Through the forms and spaces of several key building complexes, it is clear that Maki has found his own reality and would rather that we experience his architecture and urban designs and enjoy their spaces than ponder the visions and experiments that may never be.

229

230

In Reyner Banham's book, *Megastructure, Urban Futures of the Recent Past,* he relies heavily on Maki's early writing to define and articulate the megastructure. There is even an appendix called "Maki on Megastructure," which quotes from Maki's book, *Investigations in Collective Form,* published in 1964 at Washington University in St. Louis. The quotations are accurate and they provide a clear statement of the concept of the megastructure as it was understood in 1964. It is incorrect, however, to believe that Maki subscribed to that concept then or now. His

early articles with Masato Otaka on Collective Form reveal a general suspicion and dissatisfaction with the megastructure concept. His recent writing has been even more outspoken in his disappointment with the dream of technology. Essentially, Maki remains a conservative designer. Schooled in the traditions of Gropius and Sert at Harvard, and a fond believer in the subtle elegance of the traditional Japanese post-and-beam aesthetic, Maki's finest work evokes the Germanic simplicity of a modern-day Bauhaus. His involvement with the Metabolist move-

ment has always been one of polite skepticism. He employs technology as a vehicle to achieve a design solution, rather than as an end in itself.

As of this writing, Maki and Associates is engaged in the design of several projects, including the National Museum of Modern Art in Kyoto, a new-town development of 50,000 for Kanazawa, Yokohama, and a major sports complex in Kota Kinabalu, the capital of Sabah, in East Malaysia.

228, 229.
National Aquarium: Large high-strength, laminated plastic enclosures create a vast "slice of the sea" for viewing exhibitions.
230.
Site Prefab Sketch, Fumihiko Maki, 1975: From top: Osaka Prefectural Sports Center, Tsukuba University, and the National Aquarium. All three projects included on-site prefabrication for economy and ease of erection, rather than a devotion to some abstract Metabolist doctrine concerning prefabrication and interchangeability of parts.
231, 234.
Site Prefab System, National Aquarium.
232, 233.
Site Plan and Axonometric, National Aquarium.

232

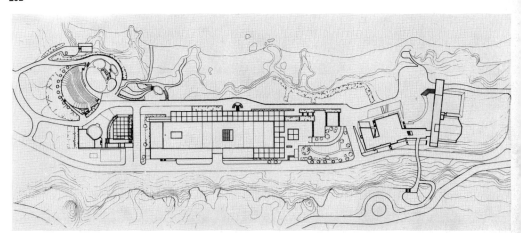

233

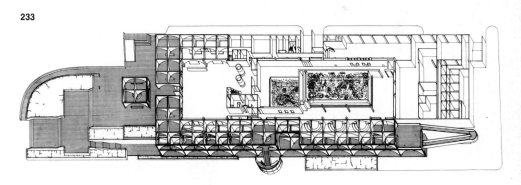

231

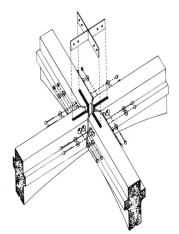

234

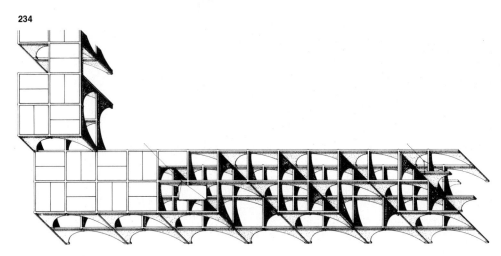

Arata Isozaki: Consciously Mannerist

One of the most bizarre, antitraditional, and important architects in Japan today is Arata Isozaki. A graduate of Tokyo University and one of the key designers on Tange's staff during the late fifties and early sixties, Isozaki played a major role in the evolution of the megastructure idea, in the Plan for Tokyo 1960, and in the conceptual design process that led to the Ya-manashi Communications Center and the plan for Skopje, Yugoslavia. After publishing several urban design schemes of his own, he established the Arata Isozaki Atelier in 1958.

His early work was bold, brutal, and without subtlety. The Oita Prefectural Library, 1966, was an expressionist interplay of heavy reinforced-concrete forms that established Isozaki as a deft sculptor of public spaces. A major departure from the technological implications of the City in the Sky sketches, the Oita Library revealed Isozaki's interest in primary forms and shaping spaces. An eclectic architect of enormous intellect, Isozaki is continually investigating and digesting aspects of foreign cultures past and present. He admits having a fondness for the work of Claude Ledoux whose simple spheres, cubes and pyramids were as refreshing and unexpected in the eighteenth century as are Isozaki's forms and spaces in this century.

235

The sixties were marked by the development of an aesthetic system employed primarily in the design of several branch banks and residences, by studies of computer-aided urban complexes, and by his wry wit. In the Festival Plaza at Expo '70, Isozaki created a computer-operated robot which, he explained, "produced light, color, sound, smell and fog. It was a robot that could walk and dance by himself." Isozaki has all but given up the thought of ever realizing the plug-in concept of his City in the Sky sketches. He says that, "I never believed in technology as the answer, although I am very interested in studying man-made things. I am very concerned with the aesthetic aspects of architecture: space, feeling and concept." His use of computers is part pleasure, part fantasy, but not the Metabolist intention of making technocratic cities. As his own words imply, his primary concern is with the aesthetic aspects of architecture. This is clearly illustrated in the evolution of branch banks for Fukuoka Sogo Bank. Both the Oita and the Daimyo branches,

237

235.
Oita Prefectural Library, Arata Isozaki, 1966: Bold brutalism and pure geometric forms dominated Isozaki's first independent projects, typical of Japanese architecture in the early 60s.
236, 237.
Fukuoka Sogo Bank, Oita Branch, Arata Isozaki, 1967: This creative, sculptural branch bank illustrates Isozaki's fascination with clerestory lighting, technological imagery, visual reflections and ambiguity in architecture.
238.
Fukuoka Sogo Bank, Daimyo Branch, Arata Isozaki, 1969: A continuation of the concepts introduced in the Oita Branch, Isozaki again employs shifted grids, clerestory lighting and expressionist air diffusers.

236

238

completed in the late sixties, employ shifted grids in plan, clerestory lighting, and a playful use of expressionist air diffusers. The pleasure of visiting both is, however, in Isozaki's manipulation of space; in his use of light and reflections to bring an element of surprise and whimsy to the mundane task of cashing a check. More recently, his branch banks in Nagasumi, Ropponmatsu and Saga are more consciously Mannerist employing a continuous grid over all the surfaces. Isozaki has noted that:

"By covering the entire composition with this membrane, divided into basic, all-pervading units, it is possible to express endless amplification in three directions because everything resolves into this framework, in which positional relations may be subjected to all kinds of changes."

Careful inspection of these projects reveals a form of graph paper wrapping its way around every surface, and pervading the entire design process. It is much more than a modular coordination-grid familiar to designers using prefabrication systems.

It is the conceptual notion that one begins with a pure, abstract, non-directional field in which walls, floors, and ceilings represent merely planes in space. Into this field the architect can project differing objects, can stretch the grid using false perspective, or can manipulate space using the grid for reference points. One interesting result of this preoccupation with squares, is that visitors may lose their orientation, confusing left with right and top with bottom. This is part of the capricious humor we have come to associate with the work of Isozaki.

239

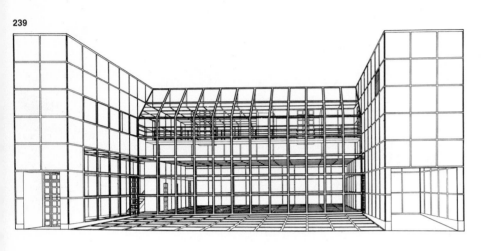

240

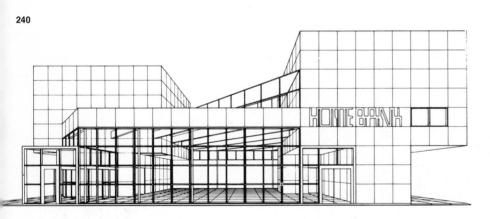

241

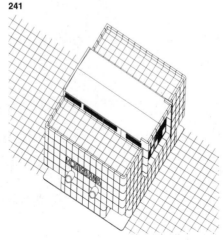

239–241.
Fukuoka Sogo Bank, Branch Bank Studies, Arata Isozaki, 1971: Isozaki's interminable interest in the cube and the amplification of square grids was first clearly established in these branch banks: Nagasumi Branch (239), Saga Branch (240) and Ropponmatsu Branch (241). He first employed clusters of cubes in the Dr. N Residence of 1964, and has continued to explore the potential of the square grid in recent projects.

242, 243.
Axonometric and Section, Oita Medical Hall, Arata Isozaki, 1960 and 1972: The semi-circular stepped portion was added twelve years after the initial building, tripling the volume. The old building is connected to the new wing by a sloping skylight creating an ambiguous inside/outside facade. (See color plate 183.)

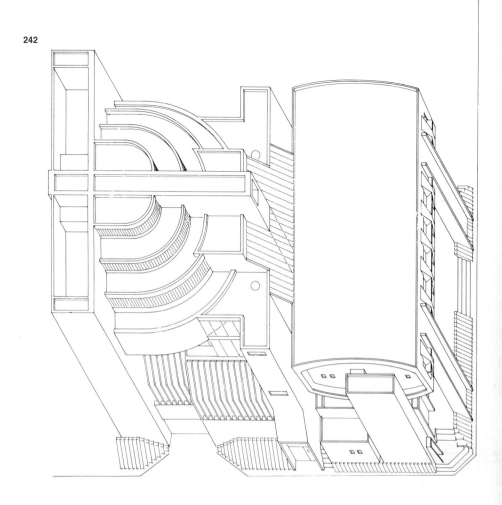

242

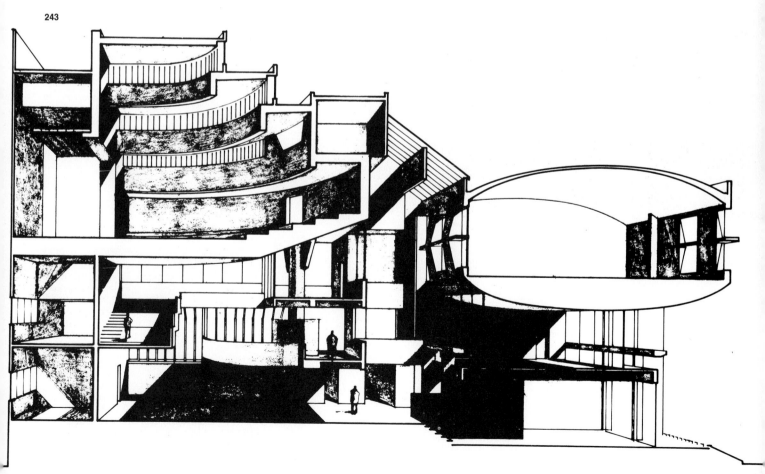

243

His skill as a manipulator of spaces is perhaps best illustrated by the Oita Medical Hall. Phase one was completed in 1960. Phase two was designed 12 years later to triple the volume of the original building. The entire project was completed in 1972. The first phase was a brutal, truncated cylinder lying on its side, supported by massive columns. At the terminus of a broad street, it stood its ground like a large fossilized mastedon. The second phase is far more skillfully handled and is joined successfully to phase one with a sloping glass skylight which transforms the previous exterior facade to an interior wall. This begins a pleasant sequence of contradictions and ambiguities. The interior is a carved-out, stepped and curving evolution of spatial experiences. Isozaki explains that he was trying to achieve the Japanese concept of *kehai,* in which you can feel someone's presence without being able to see that person. This is possible because of the openness of the whole building. The culmination of the visit is the semi-circular main conference hall. At the entry the visitor finds himself on a platform with about a seven-foot ceiling overhead. From within this space, the floor and ceiling both telescope into an open, spacious room. As the floor steps down, the clerestory ceiling steps up in a physical reflection as if some imaginary mirror were floating in the center of the space. The entire building becomes a carefully orchestrated sequence of experiences in which one is never certain of where one floor level ends and the next begins, as he follows the bridges, steps, and platforms toward his final destination.

244–247.
Oita Medical Hall: Stepped and curving forms with multiple openings create intriguing contradictions and spatial surprises. Neon tubes delineate the underside of the connecting bridge (245), which links the elevator with the stepped reading platforms (246). From across the bridge the visitor looks back, through the transparent interior window to the original exterior facade (247), which Isozaki has skillfully integrated with the new addition in a playful example of Both/And architecture.

248.
Conference Room, Oita Medical Hall: The stepped
seating platform is reflected by the stepped clerestory
ceiling as the volume telescopes open to the rostrum.

248

249–251.
Fukuoka Sogo Bank, Headquarters, Arata Isozaki, 1972: "Complexity and contradiction" are alive and well in the architecture of Isozaki. The scenic railway, with its exaggerated exhaust pipes (250) seems about to tear away from the massive stolid wall which offers the stability we associate with major financial institutions. The front facade (251) is a collection of individualized objects, set against the large flat wall. (See color plate 184.)

252–254.
Interiors, Fukuoka Sogo Bank, Headquarters: Isozaki believes each element should have its own identity, be it the main floor seating area (252), the semi-circular, marble phone booth (253), or the private reception room (254) that Isozaki designed as a cube with all six surfaces composed of concentric squares.

Immediately following the design of the Oita Medical Hall, Isozaki began work on the headquarters building of the Fukuoka Sogo Bank. In it the concept of Mannerism in architecture is most prominent. Wylie Sypher described Renaissance Mannerism as being, "marked by disproportion, disturbed balance, ambiguity, and clashing impulses."[56] It was a response to the equilibrium, exact proportions, and stability of High-Renaissance architecture. Similarly in the twentieth century, architects like Isozaki are react-

249

250

ing to the purity and stability of the articulated, logical, and possibly oversimplified designs prevalent in the sixties and early seventies, in which the corporate International Style had reduced the principles of modern architecture to simple grids and rectangular boxes *ad nauseam.*

In the Fukuoka Sogo Bank the divergence between the philosophies of Fumihiko Maki and Arata Isozaki become most apparent. Maki believes in designs in which, "each part is a small realized whole and in which the composite whole is suggested by its parts." Isozaki believes in the contrary notion that each fragment should express itself and the function it performs, and should not necessarily imply the whole. He states that each element should be handled "as an individual thing, designed to conform only to its own circumstance and unrelated to the whole. In other words, this is a conscious rejection of the universal space in favor of an aggregation of fragments. While discarding the idea of parts divided from the whole, this approach refuses to infer the whole from the parts."

From the exterior, the building is a large, red wall holding together a collection of diverse elements, not unlike Le Corbusier's Cité de Refuge (Salvation Army Building), built in Paris in 1933. The heavy, stolid quality of the red wall is contrasted by some futurist, glass-roofed vehicle parked in front, with huge exhaust pipes, about to pull out down the block.

251

252

253

254

In the interior the visitor may get off the elevator in a corridor painted jet black with a series of individually designed rooms on either side. One such room designed by Isozaki is essentially a cube with concentric squares on all six surfaces. The center of the squares is a small square mirror. From certain angles one appears to be seeing into the adjacent space, and all the while there persists this uncertainty about which surface is a wall and which is the floor and ceiling. Isozaki describes the building as, "not formal, not rigid, not consistent, mixed up, complex and ambiguous."

Another space, used for multilingual conferences, is painted completely silver. The guests sit around a large, circular table while, from within symmetrical baroque, silver, and glass corners, the interpreters simultaneously translate Japanese into a host of foreign tongues. The window to another room is draped with an over-scaled, penetrating eye designed by the Dada artist Man Ray. The entire edifice

255

256

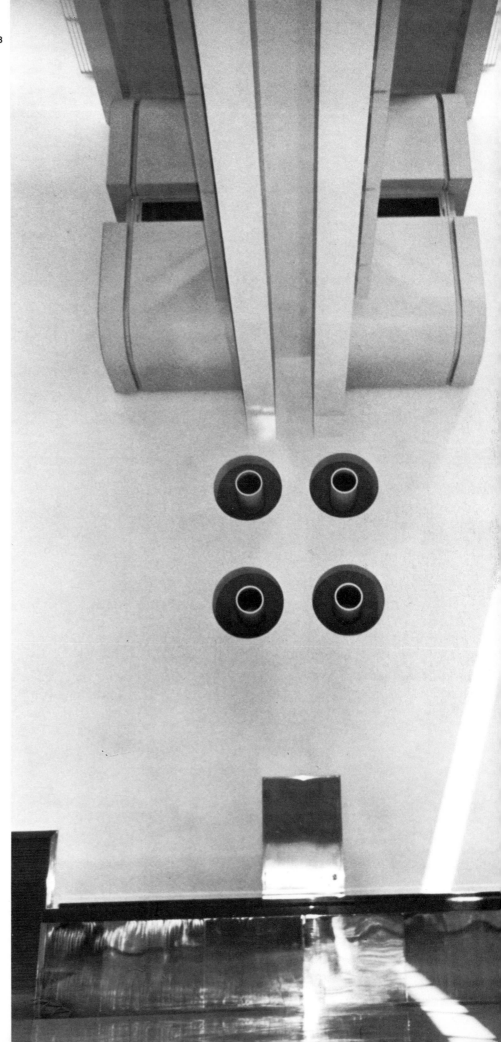

255.
International Conference Room, Fukuoka Sogo Bank, Headquarters: The two symmetrical, convex silver rooms are intended for interpreters. Each chair is equipped with headsets in order that negotiations can be carried on in several languages simultaneously.
256.
Guest Dining Room, Fukuoka Sogo Bank, Headquarters: The steady gaze of the eye by Dada artist Man Ray reminds us that perhaps "Big Brother" really is watching.
257, 258.
Interiors, Fukuoka Sogo Bank, Headquarters: General office staff conference area (257) employs ductwork, conduits and computer graphics as decoration. The main entrance lobby (258), is a symmetrical tour de force of expressionist forms.

259–261.
Gunma Prefectural Museum of Fine Arts, Arata Isozaki, 1974: Conceived as clusters of continuous cubes wrapped in a skin of squares. The cubes are bent, shifted, lifted and otherwise skillfully manipulated in the rich layers of spaces created by Isozaki.

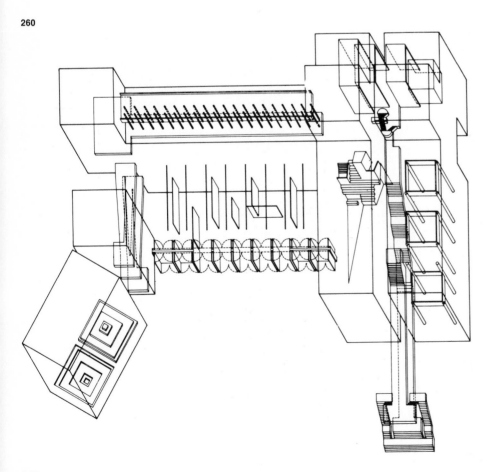

has the quality of a James Bond classic, complete with private meeting rooms accessible by a single bridge, computer graphics the size of a man, and a marble telephone booth, 12 ft (3.7 m.) in diameter.

In more recent projects Isozaki has integrated his Mannerist tendencies with his interest in the all-pervading square grid. At both the Gunma Prefectural Museum of Fine Arts and the Kitakyushu Municipal Museum of Art, Isozaki has transformed the square to encompass clusters of continuous cubes, which are then extended, bent, lifted, and shifted to achieve the spatial configuration that he is seeking. In one visit that we made to the Gunma Museum, Isozaki explained that one element, composed of a double cube, was shifted to enclose the front grounds and to give special emphasis to the traditional Japanese sculpture that was to be displayed within it. This diagonal section is a very formal space divided into two squares, each with a plaza of concentric squares. In one plaza the squares recede into the ground plane; in the second they rise to form a stepped pedestal. Although identical in plan, the spatial quality of the two adjacent plazas is distinctly different. One is positive and the other negative, a manifestation of Isozaki's mannerist impressionism.

261

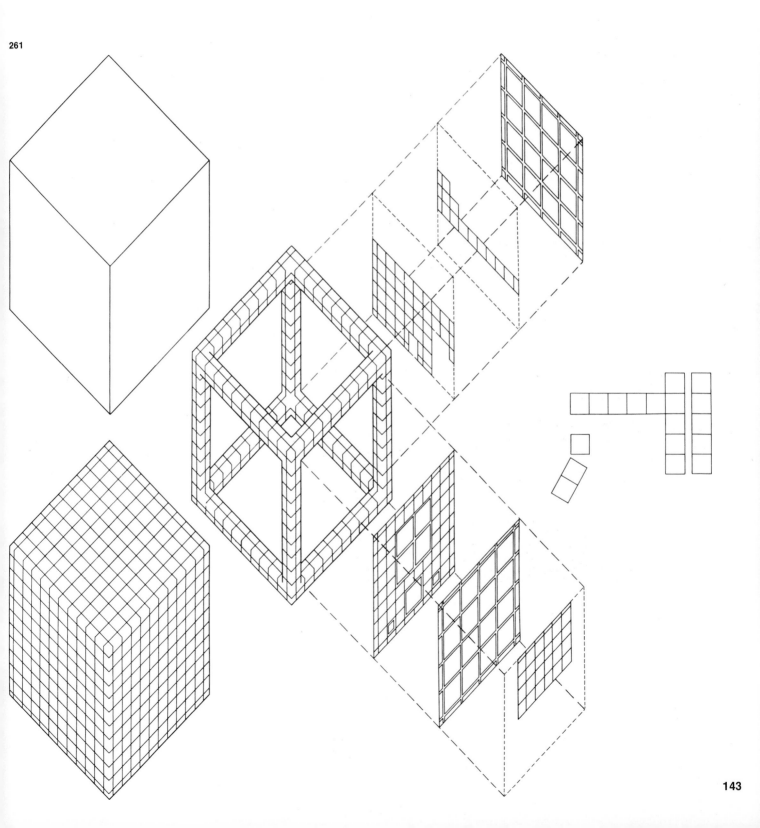

262.
Gunma Prefectural Museum of Fine Arts: The polished
aluminum square panels wrap the building in a neutral
grid which is then massaged and distorted to create
multiple readings and ambiguous metaphors.

263, 264.
Central Hall, Gunma Prefectural Museum: The focus of this axial space is a large stepped volume which reads as a major staircase, rendered even more prominent in perspective by the converging grids. It is in fact a grandiose set of display platforms, a super-juxtaposition of two different scales, which parodies architectural logic.

265–267.
Kitakyushu Municipal Museum of Art, Arata Isozaki, 1975: Cubes extruded into box-beams dominate the hillside in bold expressionism, lacking the subtle sophistication of the Gunma Prefectural Museum.

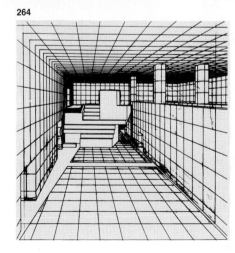

At the Kitakyushu Municipal Museum of Art, Isozaki employs cubes extruded into two surreal box-beams which overshadow the landscape. This assertive expressionist massing can be seen earlier in the square concrete beams of the Oita Prefectural Library, 1966, and the two box-beams flanking either side of the Fukuoka Sogo Bank Headquarters building completed in 1972.

The origins of these forms are uncertain, but their continual reappearance in Isozaki's work suggests an interest in creating architecture of great mass and gravity. It's a virile architecture which asserts its presence rather than trying to evoke a sense of contextualism as was apparent in the work of Fumihiko Maki. These same defiant metal-clad extrusions, which dominate the exterior of the Kitakyushu Museum, penetrate into the large central entrance hall with unrelenting power, softened only by the gently curving marble handrails and the delicate quality of the clerestory lighting. It is high drama, but there is some question as to whether it is truly high art.

265

266

267

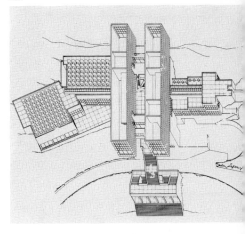

Peter Cook of Archigram has said of Isozaki that he is "A designer who exploits the total expressionist range available, whether inside architecture or just outside."[57] This picture aptly describes the continuously changing and stimulating architectural design that the Arata Isozaki Atelier has been consistently producing in recent years. Both the Gunma and Kitakyushu Museums modulate light, form, and space to dramatize the display of art and to charge the buildings with a kind of electricity that energizes the people in them. At the Gunma Museum the central hall is filled with an oversized stair ostensibly for people, but the false perspective belies its true scale and purpose, which is for the display of sculpture. One is reminded of Michelangelo's stair in the Laurentian Library anteroom, which also fills its space. Wylie Sypher suggests that perhaps Michelangelo "had intended to parody architectural logic" and that, "Michelangelo was the first to turn architecture into a medium for individual expression."[58] Both of these qualities—individual expressionism and the parody of architectural logic—are paramount in Isozaki's twentieth-century Mannerism.

268

268.
Main Hall, Kitakyushu Municipal Museum of Art: The defiant, metal-clad extrusions penetrate through the dramatic main entry, which is softened only by the curved, marble handrails and the clerestory lighting.
269.
Kitakyushu Central Library, Arata Isozaki, 1975: Isozaki digresses from the square only as far as the circle. The curved, vaulted forms represent a creative departure from the geometric purity of Claude Ledoux, one of Isozaki's strongest influences. Isozaki's interest in curved surfaces and circular volumes dates back to his earliest projects and appears in various forms throughout his career. More recent examples of this interest in vaulted volumes can be seen in the Yano Residence and the Fujimi Country Club House.

269

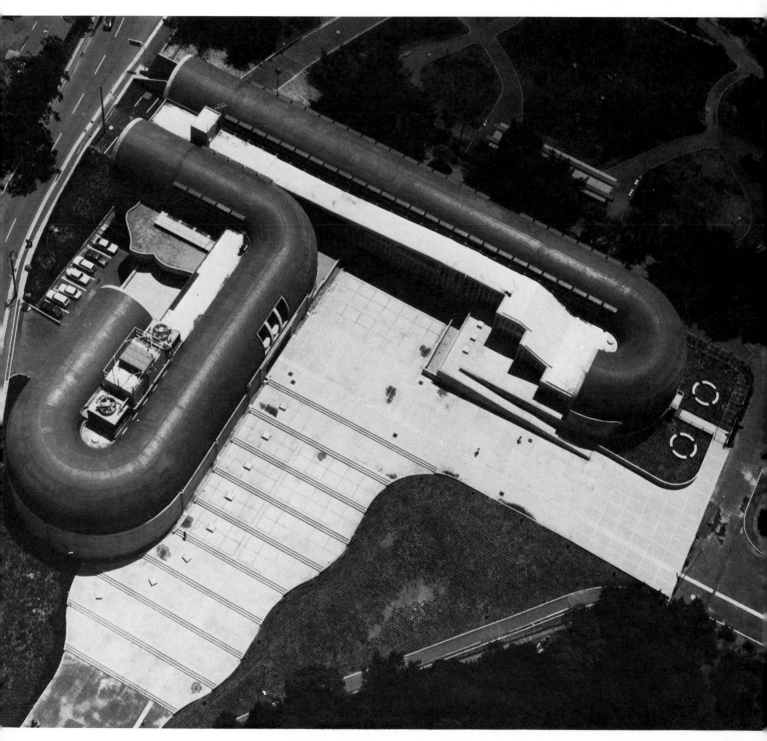

Minoru Takeyama: Northern Radical

Born March 15, 1934, in Sapporo, capital city of Japan's northernmost island, Hokkaido, Minoru Takeyama has remained a child of the north, a pioneer in a nation founded on tradition. Takeyama calls Hokkaido "the California of Japan." It's that far-off precinct, the last area to be tamed, and the most unconventional. He points out that Hokkaido declared itself independent from Japan in 1868 during the start of the Meiji restoration. The state of independence lasted a brief two weeks, but the sense of individualism remains more than one hundred years later.

While his architecture may seem unconventional and his mood may be that of a pioneer, his credentials are unsurpassed. Takeyama graduated with a Master's degree from the School of Architecture, Waseda University, in 1958, and attended Harvard on a Fulbright Scholarship, from which he graduated in 1960. He remained in America until 1962, working with a variety of outstanding designers including Jose Luis Sert, Hideo Sasaki, and Isamu Noguchi. After nearly three years in the United States, Takeyama moved to Denmark where he worked for Jørn Utzon on the Sidney Opera House. When Utzon left for Australia in 1963, Takeyama worked for Arne Jacobsen, and later with Henning Larsen. Together Larsen and Takeyama won second prize in the Berlin Free University competition. In 1964 he returned to Tokyo and opened his own office—Minoru Takeyama & The United Actions. After a succession of restaurants, interiors and houses, Takeyama captured the at-

270.
Ichibankan (left) and Nibankan, Minoru Takeyama, 1969 and 1970: Like abstract paintings, the building names translate simply to "Building Number One" and "Building Number Two." (See color plate 185.)

271.
Ichibankan: Is it a black rocketship or a techno-layercake? Takeyama's wit and skill converge in this playful urban symbol of the future, whose shiny skin encloses a stack of pubs, cafes and cabarets.

272.
Pepsi-Cola® Canning Plant, Minoru Takeyama, 1972: The glass drum supported by vertical trusses forms a powerful symbol of modern technology in the rural Hokkaido landscape. (See color plate 187.)

273.
National Aquarium, Kevin Roche, John Dinkeloo and Associates, 1966: The partial cylinder with sloping roof enclosed in glass was, Takeyama admits, a good idea that needed to be built.

271

270

tention of the architectural world with his Ichibankan in 1969, and Nibankan in 1970. Like abstract paintings, the building names translate simply to "Building number one" and "Building number two."

Both structures are geometric, bold, and abstract, exhibiting the influence of his years with Noguchi. Yet they are also a parody of high art. Like Isozaki, whose roots are in Kyushu, Japan's southernmost island, Takeyama remains a third-generation child of Hokkaido, doubting the intellectualism of urban Tokyo and

opting instead for a lampoon of traditional architectural principles. The truncated building profile of Ichibankan follows the silhouette of the Tokyo zoning laws, while the high central circulation space Takeyama claims is a vertical extension of the street. The building department ruled that this portion of the structure came under the jurisdiction of the J.I.S. (Japan Industrial Standards) and therefore required stripes to warn low-flying aircraft of its presence. In response to this requirement, Takeyama covered the entire surface with a layer cake of stripes, claiming he was,

"making fun of regulations through my own interpretation." The surface of the building is a mixture of inexpensive, prefabricated materials selected from a catalogue. The central space is clad in reflective silver glass creating a high-tech, cubist spaceship by day, and a glowing series of intimate cafes and pubs during Japan's religiously observed happy hour, which begins after work and lasts until about midnight. The irony of a building which appears to be one thing and turns out to be entirely other than what one expects, is part of the surprise and schizo-phrenia of Takeyama's architecture.

This is most apparent in his Pepsi-Cola® Canning Plant in Mikasa, Hokkaido, completed in 1972. Located in the rural farmland of his native prefecture, Takeyama was determined to avoid building what looked like a factory. Instead, he again chose a highly technological, simple, geometric enclosure which brought ample light to the factory workers, was relatively inexpensive, and easy to erect. He admits being influenced by the Roche and Dinkeloo aquarium project for Washington, D.C., which also envisioned a large cylindrical space with sloping roof enclosed in glass. Takeyama's design, however, has been adapted to its function, creating a symbolic contradiction. In a climate where six feet of snowfall is commonplace, he sloped the roof toward a central boiler room which melts the snow, sending forth a mysterious cloudy mist. From a distance, it appears that Pepsi-Cola® is made from Japanese snow in a big boiler. Takeyama loves the irony of the whole project. In addition to producing 1,000 cans per minute of one of America's best-kept se-

crets, the building serves its community as a cultural center. Future additions will include an auditorium, a museum, and a laboratory. An artificial earth berm encircling the building visually guards the factory machinery from view, creating a pure sculpture in the landscape. The visual presence of the building is so strong that Pepsi® reportedly canceled a whole year's planned publicity in a weekly magazine.

The two production lines of the Pepsi-Cola® canning process were accommodated simply and economically, but with-

274.
Interior, Pepsi-Cola® Canning Plant.
275, 276.
Hotel Beverly Tom, Minoru Takeyama, 1973: Some obvious phallic symbolism, rising to a technological summit climaxes Takeyama's tongue-in-cheek addition to the industrial center at Tomakomai.

276

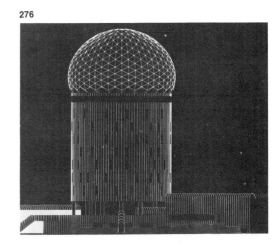

275

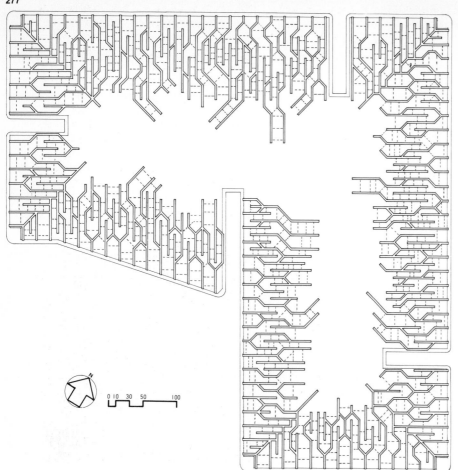

out a conventional solution. Takeyama's concept was to wrap the required machinery in a simple surface that did not inhibit nor impede their function, yet allowed him the freedom to make design decisions based on how the building should look from the outside. The function does not produce the form, nor does the form inhibit the function. In a sense, they are distinct and separate issues, as long as they both work. Fortunately, in this case, they do. Pepsi-Cola® got their sales symbol and the factory workers have a brighter, more pleasant environment in which to work; but there persists a nag-

277–282.
Housing Collectivity, Minoru Takeyama, 1974: A mixture of fireproof concrete walls (277) covered by a lattice of plywood box units (278, 279) creates a labyrinthine residential fabric similar in scale and texture to traditional Japanese villages. Typical of Japanese architechnology, the box units flip, flop, rotate and adjust to a multitude of situations (280–282).

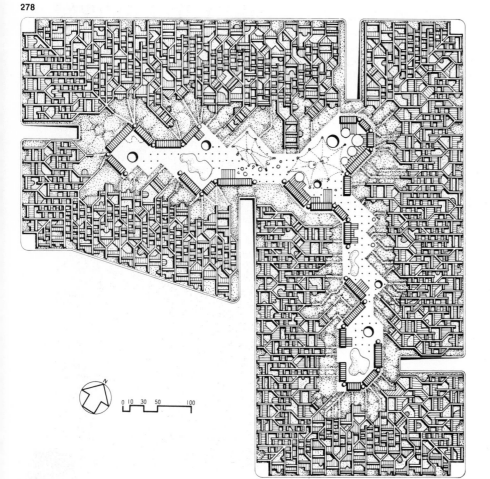

ging feeling that Takeyama is playing too much the visual gamesman. His buildings drift dangerously close to the edge of the techno-aesthetic, in which the facade of technology is more important than the substance of the architecture. This is perhaps most apparent in the Hotel Beverly Tom.

The Hotel Beverly Tom, completed in 1973, is a logical extension of the concepts inherent in the Pepsi-Cola® Canning Plant. It also is a three-quarter circle in plan, rising to a highly technological summit. The dome at the top of the ten-story lobby was designed with the assistance of Shoji Sadao, a disciple and frequent coauthor of projects by Buckminster Fuller.

Located in Tomakomai, an industrial center on the island of Hokkaido, the building sits at the edge of the expanding industrial development, looking toward the natural terrain and mountains that were once the sole masters of this northern province. Against the dark, desolate townscape of oil tanks and railroad yards, the Hotel Beverly Tom is a phallic symbol of what technology can produce.

The black metal skin of the hotel is a parody on the stark, cylindrical oil tanks in the surrounding landscape, and with its dome at the top, dominates the horizon. It is true that the view from the dome is magnificent, but the question remains, was this obvious symbolism really necessary, and what purpose does it serve? It does serve, I suppose, to create a landmark out of what might have been a commonplace collection of hotel rooms, but more importantly it serves as another stage on which Takeyama can perform his aesthetic acrobatics. A skillful designer enjoys the use of symbolic gesture in ar-

280

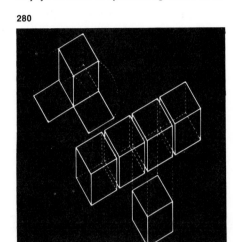

281

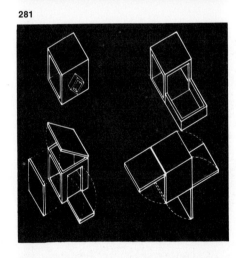

282

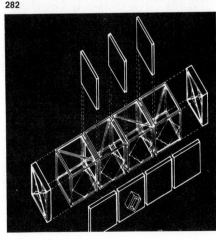

279

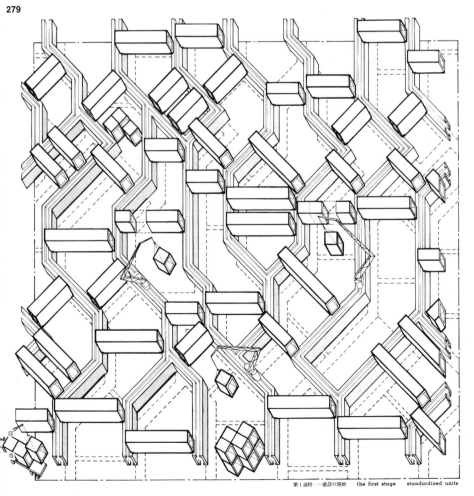

第1過程——建設の開始　the first stage　standardized units

155

chitecture, but in the case of the Hotel Beverly Tom the symbolism is a bit too transparent.

More recently, Takeyama has turned his flair for fusing fantasy with function toward the development of a low-rise, high-density residential system which is a more successful integration of concept and context. Since the client was a large lumber company, Takeyama was compelled to use as much wood as the building code would allow. He developed a two-layer system, employing an earth layer of concrete as the base with a particle-board

system of cubes resting above.

The semipublic space between the units Takeyama refers to as the "twilight zone," part private and part public. This twilight zone forms the basic physical structure of the system defining circulation patterns and acting as the channels which carry the infrastructure. Bridging this labyrinthine network of spaces are Takeyama's prefabricated wooden cubes. Each cube is about 8 ft (2.4 m) on a side, which can form a sleeping module, or the cubes can be clustered to form larger spaces. Optional components include hinged panels

which drop down forming a balcony or bridge to another space. To test the versatility of the system, Takeyama is building an eight-cube studio in Sapporo which he plans to rearrange at regular intervals. He is intrigued with the idea of a kinetic architecture which is composed of the same basic images, but is capable of achieving a variety of forms. Like homonyms, which present the same image at face value but which have different meanings, Takeyama refers to his design concept as "homology," in which different forms can be made from objects having the same basic image. To some extent it is a game of semantics, but it is an attempt to articulate a visual system using a foreign language and, to a certain extent, it can be edifying.

Minoru Takeyama & The United Actions has realized a simplified version of this residential system which Takeyama believes could form the first increment of a larger, more complex total community, like the one envisioned in his original scheme. The prototype house employs the same two-layer system of perpendicular tubes, square in section, which overlap a concrete base to form open and closed semiprivate interior spaces. The intricate interlocking of spaces in the proposed larger complex is a skillful reinterpretation of the qualities of community and privacy that existed in the traditional Japanese village.

Takeyama's career continues to be a cycle of research, experimentation, and implementation. In the summer of 1975 he visited the United States to continue his research into the semeiology of streets, examining the influence of visual signs on the urban fabric. Back in Japan, he has joined what he implies may become the next Metabolist Group, called ArchiteXt.

[*sic*] Composed of Takefumi Aida, Takamitsu Azuma, Mayumi Miyawaki, Makoto Suzuki, and Minoru Takeyama, the group is examining alternative design methods in the hopes of creating a new integration of art and technology.[59] To date, their work reflects primarily the attitude of *l'enfant terrible* trying outrageous departures from the norm to attract attention, more than anything else. ArchiteXt and Takeyama together represent a trend in Japan away from the traditional toward the experimentation and pizazz of an Archigram or Archizoom,[60] from which the group evolved their own ambiguous appellation.

284

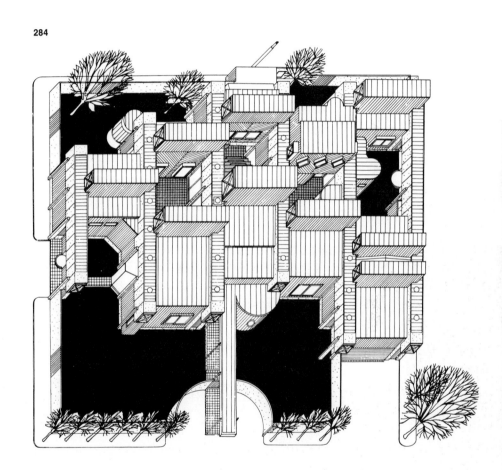

283, 284.
Prototypical Residence, Minoru Takeyama, 1974: Based on the Housing Collectivity System, the parallel walls and perpendicular box units are the form generators of this experiment in ''kinetic'' architecture.

Shin'ichi Okada: Son of the Big Five

It has long been an accepted practice in Japan that once an architect enters the employ of one of the Big Five design-build conglomerates, he will remain with that company until his retirement. This arrangement assures both parties of security, loyalty and lifelong dependence. Only a person of rare and extraordinary talents ever departs from one of the Big Five to achieve individual recognition. These exceptional qualities are part of the growth and eventual departure of Shin'ichi Okada

from the design division of Kajima Corporation.

Born in Tokyo in 1928, Okada received his Bachelor and Master of Architecture degrees from Tokyo University and entered the design division of Kajima Corporation in 1957. Several years later, as one of Kajima's most promising designers, he entered the Graduate School of Yale University. After graduating in 1963 at the age of 35, Okada began working for Skidmore, Owings and Merrill. In 1964 he returned to the Kajima Corporation as one of their chief designers. During the late sixties

285

Okada won several design awards including one for the Home Office building of Kajima Corporation, the first high-rise building in Japan to employ a precast concrete curtain wall. In 1969 he was awarded first place in the national competition for the new Supreme Court Building. Winning this competition afforded Okada the opportunity to open his own architectural practice. He departed Kajima on good terms, sparing them the embarrassment of having their chief designer working on a project outside the office. Since 1969, Okada's practice has continued to prosper, and today he is considered one of the more successful designers in Japan.

Shin'ichi Okada's mentors were Paul Rudolph and Louis Kahn. His work shows the influence of Rudolph's bold massing and Kahn's geometric simplicity, prevalent throughout his career, but Okada rarely exhibits the grace and charm of Kahn's mature work. The home office of Kajima Corporation indicates Okada's early interest in shifting masses to achieve slices of space in tension between large, heavy solids. The two office towers are shifted in plan, creating an entry slot which receives visitors from a broad plaza. The plaza itself is a pleasant sanctuary which steps down from the busy street in a series of terraces, like an open Japanese fan. Okada has designed the sequence of spaces from street to office to be a far more interesting and less intimidating experience than most high-rise blocks, which are simply set on an open deck. The stepped-down plaza at Kajima contains a fountain which performs the familiar task of masking street noise. As the visitor moves from the plaza into the building, he is received by a large, two-story lobby which opens on a private garden. This sense of openness is maintained at each

285–287.
Kajima Corporation, Headquarters Building, Shin'ichi Okada and Kajima Corporation, 1968 and 1971: The twin towers, built three years apart, are connected by bridges made famous by Kenzo Tange and the Metabolists. Shifted in plan, the towers form an entry plaza between them.

287

286

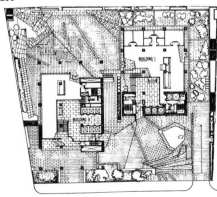

elevator landing by the use of paired floors, which create two-story spaces. The banks of elevators are located at the towers' periphery affording the visitor a broad panoramic view of the city as he steps off the elevator. The two towers are connected by three bridges in the sky, echoing earlier megastructures by Kenzo Tange and the Metabolist Group.

The Supreme Court Building
The competition for the Supreme Court Building was won in 1969 and the building was completed in March 1974. The spaces within the building are formed by large

288

walls. These monumental slabs of stone have been labeled "space walls" by Okada, because they contain slices of space within their mass, varying from 13–20 ft (4–6 m) in width. The over-all massing of the building is reminiscent of Rudolph's concrete structure at the Yale Art and Architecture Building, but the basic design concept is derived from Kahn's notion of separate "served and servant" spaces. Each space wall is a servant space housing the elevators, stairs, pantries, machine rooms, pipe-and-duct spaces, and corridors. These servant spaces articulate and separate the diverse functions within the building. This is similar to the distinc-

tion between served and servant spaces depicted most clearly in Kahn's Richards Medical Center and the Salk Institute for Biological Studies.

Okada's design philosophy is, in essence, a paraphrasing of Kahn's. He explains that, "For the designer, the work process consists in having an over-all image of the total project and at the same time dealing with his mental image and with purely practical details . . . by 'image' I mean something that goes almost as deeply as the 'form' of Louis Kahn."[61] Okada's ability to translate his image into an integrated

289

290

291

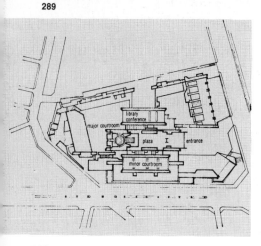

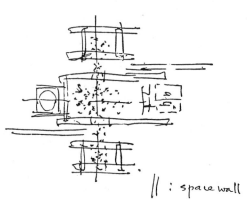

work of architecture, while considerable, falls far short of the directness and visual power of Kahn's work. However, he suffers from the same oversimplification which diminishes the effect of some of Kahn's buildings. Kahn once said that, "I think architects should be composers and not designers. They should be composers of elements."[62] Undoubtedly one of America's great architectural composers, Kahn's desire to compose or arrange elements is perhaps the basic weakness in certain of his buildings, and is the underlying problem with Okado's Supreme Court Building.

The exterior is a composition of rough-surfaced, granite-faced walls, which won the hearts of the judges, but became a rigid mold within which Okada had to develop his final solution. Okada was aware of the problem caused by winning the competition. He has said that, "Because a group of judges selected my design, I had to respect it. In a sense, it ceased to be my own."[63] He worked diligently to achieve a meaningful interior within the framework of the award-winning shell. He admits that, "the exterior of the supreme court developed too little,"[64] and he is right. It is overscaled and too simplistic. He should have developed his own design as he would any project, within the basic *parti*[65] of the space walls.

The total building does, however, work well at the urban scale. The granite walls relate well to the stone walls of the Imperial Palace moat across the street, and the hierarchy of spaces from the street through the main hall and into the various court chambers functions successfully. The main hall acts as an urban plaza, like the central public space in the Boston City

288–291.
Supreme Court, Shin'ichi Okada, 1974: Massive parallel slabs of stone define slices of space labeled "space walls" by Okada. These linear zones are based on Louis Kahn's concept of "served and servant" spaces. In this case, the space walls act as the servant spaces.

292, 293.
Interiors, Supreme Court: Geometric simplicity, smooth granite surfaces, and the dauntless use of skylights dominate the Main Hall (292) and the Major Court (293).

293

292

Hall. It is defined by the monolithic space-walls but implies an openness to the sky by use of a cylindrical ceiling curving up at its edges. Between the walls and the ceiling Okada has provided skylights which bathe the walls with natural light, suggesting an outdoor plaza. He calls this "exteriorized covered space." It represents a megascale version of the traditional Japanese *genkan,* the covered transition place between the exterior and the internal building functions. Other rooms also employ cylindrical skylights to bring light into the spaces enclosed by the solid walls.

The general impact of the building is certainly that of a monument. It is massive, bold, and imposing. Okada understands this and perceives a need for monumentality in the urban fabric. He believes that certain structures, like the Supreme Court Building, should be monumental. He defines monumentality as possessing the following qualities: "Scale that permits transmission into the future, continuity, long life, and the dream of durability in the face of change."[66] Durability in the face of change may be a useful attribute, but monumentality is not the only way to

achieve historical or enduring significance. The Katsura Detached Palace in Japan, or the Villa Savoye in the West, have withstood the changes of time without imposing the heavy-handed solution of the Supreme Court complex.

Niigata Faculty, Nippon Dental College
During the five years that Okada labored on the Supreme Court Building he had the opportunity to develop a large college campus. Without the stigmas of a competition-winning design, Okada developed a more refined solution integrating exterior

294

form with internal space planning. Located on the bleak shores of the cold northern Japan Sea in Niigata, the Nippon Dental College campus responds well to its environment and to the needs of the students and faculty who use it. The long, gray, unfriendly winters produce powdery, white salt deposits from the ocean which tend to collect on vertical panes of glass and erode untreated metal. Okada devised a system of clay-tiled vertical walls and steeply sloping glass skylights which keep out the cold, let in the bright winter sun, and shed the white salt deposits.

294.
Niigata Faculty, Nippon Dental College, Shin'ichi Okada, 1972: The influence of Kahn's Richards Medical Building is apparent in the site plan and in the use of articulated geometric masonry forms.

In plan, the clusters of connected square blocks with their protruding stair and service towers are a direct descendent of Louis Kahn's Richards Medical Building. The entire aesthetic is based on Kahn's use of masonry and his desire to create articulated mass and void, using natural light to accentuate the geometric simplicity. With the completion of phase one in late 1972, Okada realized the major portion of a campus designed to be a system of links and clusters enclosing a central campus mall. The mall is flanked on either side by a long, stepped wall of buildings

which act to define the central public space in a fashion similar to the enclosing space walls of the Supreme Court main hall. Pedestrian circulation paths across the mall serve to tie the stepped structures together. Okada calls this, "the 'tie system,' because it is a system of movement that acts to draw buildings together and causes their mutual interaction."

In each of his buildings Shin'ichi Okada has attempted to incorporate exterior space into the total design package, defining its perimeter with massive walls

shifted in plan to allow circulation at the corners. This is a spatial device used successfully by Louis Kahn and by Frank Lloyd Wright before him. Okada, through experience, is gaining dexterity and skill in his use of this aesthetic system. Judging from the success of the Niigata Faculty for the Nippon Dental College and several other projects, including the Gunma Cultural Hall, the Nagasaki Children's Center and the Kurashiki Youth Lodge, we can expect a long career of architectural competence from Shin'ichi Okada.

In order for competence to become excellence, a degree of refinement, maturity, and creative skill must be combined to produce a new order or aesthetic system in architecture. Okada remains at this point primarily a borrower, rather than an innovator. Whether he can transcend the work of his Western mentors and develop an architecture that is truly his own, one which advances the state of the art, remains to be seen.

295–297.
Niigata Faculty, Nippon Dental College: The system of stepped blocks and sloping steel skylights sheds the white salt deposits common in this ocean region and allows the penetration of warm sunlight.

297

296

5.
Futurism:
Fantasy versus Reality

A contemporary TV ad warns us that, "The future will be here in a moment. Don't let it take you by surprise." In no other culture is this warning taken more seriously than it is in Japan. Quick to borrow and learn from other cultures, after the Second World War Japan began industrializing with a vengeance. The by-now old story about how it borrowed transistor technology from the USA and rebuilt the radio, TV and communication industries is a small indicator of today's techno-society. The mass media provides a never-ending onslaught of new and better technology. Magazine and television ads foster a continuous need for the latest and most complex mechanical contrivance. Japan's favorite TV, movie, and comic book hero is *Jinzō Ningen* which loosely translates into "Techno-man." An integrated circuit of blinking lights, tubes and dials, Techno-man can overcome any obstacle and defeat any foe. True to form, the Japanese simply borrowed America's Superman and improved on him. Remember, Superman could be weakened by kryptonite, but nothing can stop Techno-man!

How Japan manages to maintain its cultural regimentation and strict order while adapting itself so readily to change is a curiosity that few can explain. This apparent contradiction was observed by Ruth Benedict as early as 1946 when she pointed out that the Japanese are "incomparably rigid in their behavior. . . . But they adapt themselves readily to extreme innovations."[67] Bernard Rudofsky also observed that, "Their genius for avoiding clear-cut solutions enables them to assimilate things foreign without budging in their old ways."[68] Whatever their secret, the Japanese are lunging headlong into the future, dragging most of their cultural traditions along with them, and mixing in a few they borrowed from us.

298, 299.
The Japanese answer to Superman is the successful comic book and cartoon hero, *Jinzō Ningen,* better known in English as "Techno-man." His crystal-clear thoughts illustrate the perfection of a technological mind.

300.
In a techno-society the onslaught of dials, buttons and gadgets are seemingly everywhere and, as the Panasonic® ad confirms, choosing just one is not easy, which is, after all, the whole idea.

301.
Sony® TV Wall: Media madness disseminates the
multiple message to the people on the Ginza and
throughout Japan.

302–305.
The Medium is the Massage: True to Marshall
McLuhan's predictions of a decade ago, "The medium
. . . electrical technology—is reshaping and
restructuring patterns of social interdependence and
every aspect of our personal life." Never more true
than in contemporary Japanese society in which the
ubiquitous boob-tube provides the fantasies of the
day: a lucite suction-cup breast builder (303), a body
bath blown from a hose (302), a voluptuous dream
(304) and a topless beauty contest (305).

301

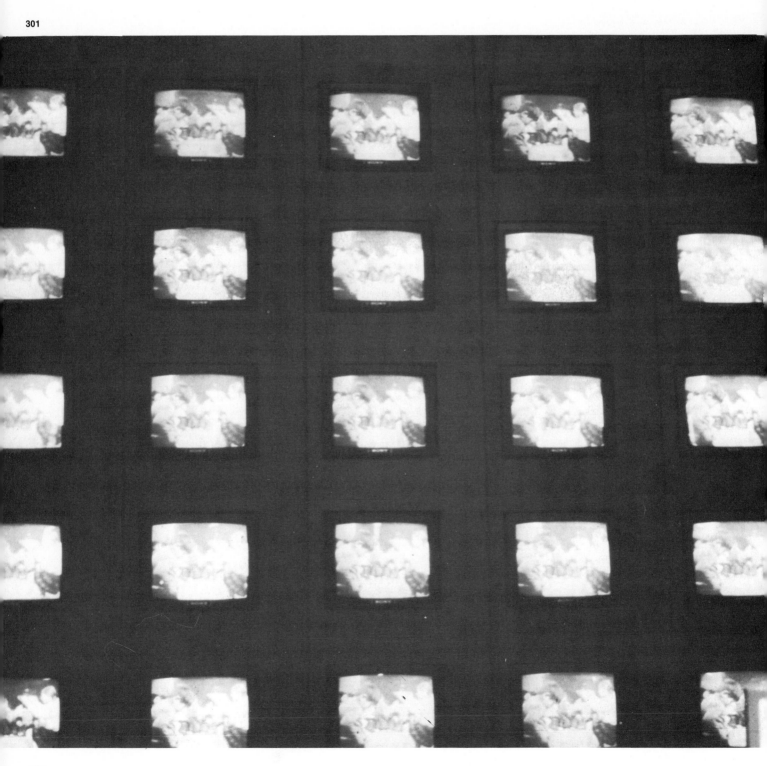

Sony® Corporation's wall of television sets, visible from the Ginza, symbolizes Japan's new fascination with technology. From these ubiquitous, omnipotent, luminous boxes issue forth the dreams, fantasies and technological wonders of the day. A lucite suction-cup breast-builder is demonstrated on a young model while a middle-aged matron in traditional kimono explains its virtues; a man realizes his dream of watching a voluptuous woman bathing; and a topless beauty contest is held, much to the embarrassment and confusion of its participants. (But don't forget the credo—to borrow and improve).

Whatever the future of the Japanese people, it will undoubtedly be that of an urban society. An island nation of extremely high density, its inhabitants long ago resolved themselves to living in cities. Architects and urbanists have therefore turned their attentions to designing these cities-of-the-future. Surrounding the techno-society described above are a proliferation of new urban forms and prototypes. Following is a preliminary outline of some of the futurist cities currently being examined and tested in Japan. It includes: Electrographic City, Computer City, Inflatable City, Floating City, Movable City, and Instant City.

Electrographic City

In 1927, Le Corbusier reminded architects that, "Our eyes are constructed to enable us to see forms in light,"[69] but he neglected to mention that the light source need not be the sun alone. The light source might be anything that emits or reflects enough light rays to register an impulse in our brain. Headlights, flashlights, traffic lights, bar signs, and neon lines are all potential materials on the architect's pallette. Few architects or urban designers in this country have attempted to deal with light as a legitimate design medium for shaping our cities.

302

304

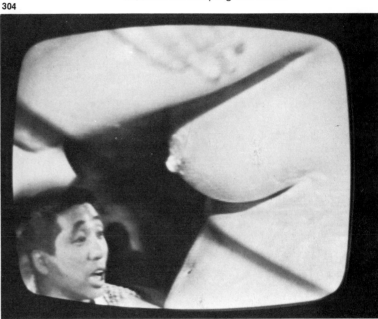

303

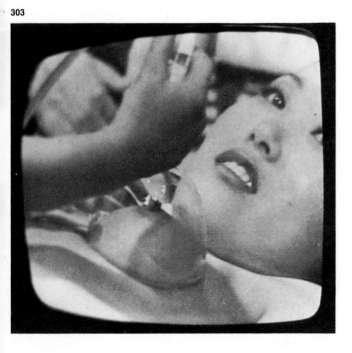

305

169

In December 1968, Tom Wolfe wrote a zany article in the Los Angeles Sunday Supplement about the wonders of Southern California sign designers. The article was reprinted in July 1969, in *Architectural Design,* entitled "Electrographic Architecture." It was a slap in the face which awoke Western architects to the latent potential of making buildings and cities out of light. Robert Venturi and Denise Scott Brown proceeded to transport their Yale protégés to Nevada in order to record and analyze the marvels of Las Vegas. It took an architect who spent his early years as a stage set-designer using lights to shape and define space, like Hugh Hardy of Hardy Holzman Pfeiffer Associates, to begin employing light as a viable architectural tool. But all American attempts at creatively integrating light into our architecture pale when compared to the luminous wonders of the Ginza, Shibuya, and Shinjuku districts of Tokyo.

The urban fabric of Tokyo is a lucid diagram of light, in which important nodes or districts achieve clarity and legibility by the nature of their electrographic presence. This presence, or "imageability" as Kevin Lynch called it, is that quality that gives these nodes their visual structure and identity. The most famous of these is the Ginza, in which light varies from a supergraphic word to an entire building. The electrographic environment may be highly structured and designed, as in the Shibuya area, or it may be a pattern of random order achieved by the superimposition of radiant rectangles, as in the Shinjuku area.

More than the mere proliferation of adver-

tising along the "Great White Way" of Times Square, or through the super-signs of Las Vegas, Japanese architects have recognized that light can be employed as a building material as much as brick, concrete, or glass. The art of making architecture with light was first captured in a single building in 1963, with the completion of the Sanai Dream Center in the heart of the Ginza. Designed by Nikken Sekkei, Ltd., it was a realization of David Crane's City Symbolic in which Crane declared, "The city should be a giant message system, or symbolic intelligence apparatus,

which provides the citizen with a simple succession of perceptible informations."[70]

Creating a pure cylinder 12 stories high on the busiest corner in the Ginza would seem to be enough of a contribution to a giant message system, but to then wrap the concrete floors with fluorescent tubes rather than spandrel glass, and to top it all off with a 50-foot-high (15.2 m) continuous fluorescent drum, achieved a piece of perceivable information that left the urban designers gazing. Of course "serious" architects ignored light as a legitimate

306.
Electrographic City: A typical street in the Shinjuku district of Tokyo. The urban forms and visual environment are completely dominated by the electrographic architecture. (See color plate 189).
307.
Sanai Dream Center, Nikken Sekkei, Ltd., 1963: The city as a "giant message system" proposed by David Crane, is alive and luminous in downtown Tokyo.

307

building material, and continued to design elegantly proportioned facades of stone and metal, only to see them masked behind the cosmetic lights of *Pachinko* parlors.[71] The tactile rhythm of neon tubing turning the corner and of continuous glowing globes gracing the entrance became as much a part of the architectural character of the building during the day as it was at night. It became apparent that to ignore the visual potential of light in key areas of the city was to ask that your building be haphazardly covered later. Accordingly, the designers of the Jintan building in Shibuya embraced the new material, coating the entire elevator and stair shaft

308, 309.
Pachinko Parlor, Shibuya District, Tokyo: During the day or the night the tactile rhythm of the neon tubes and glowing globes dominates the facade of this corner office building. The electrographic architecture becomes the urban environment and the carefully articulated glass and metal spandrel facade behind it becomes a background.
310, 311.
Jintan Building, Shibuya District, Tokyo: The integration of light-as-architecture with the traditionally blank wall of the stair and elevator tower produced this landmark building.

with a 150-foot-high (45.7 m) wall of light, topped off with a rotating rainbow of colors; another visual landmark in the giant message system.

Yoshinobu Ashihara wasn't content to light the elevator and stair shaft alone. In 1966, he designed the Sony® building, skillfully integrating multicolored lights on each floor with a changing mosaic of black and white on the service tower. This introduced the variable facade into nocturnal architectural design, the precursor of the present-day "kinetic cornice" which dominates the Tokyo skyline.

Classical facades have largely been divided into three horizontal layers: the base; the *piano nobile,* or main floor; and the cornice. The pattern can be seen from Alberti's Palazzo Ruccelai to McKim Meade and White's twentieth-century Neoclassic facades. Even Lever House and the Seagram® Building have a horizontal band at the top and the bottom which is distinct from the central portion. Contemporary Tokyo office structures depart from this pattern with the introduction of the kinetic cornice, in which the top one-third of the facade is an ever-changing visual field enclosing, of course, the elevator tower and the mechanical

equipment. From the street, the first 60% to 70% of the structure is office space as usual. Beyond that, the sky's the limit. A casual stroll through the Ginza is enough to convince anyone with his eyes open.

After the light show settles onto the retina, one is tempted to pause and ask "why here?" Are the Japanese so enamored with technology that their passion for plugging in buildings has obliterated their good sense? It is true there is a tendency in Japan to try to do their predecessors one better, but that's not really the generator for this electrographic wonderlust. It's something far more basic and traditional

310

311

to Japanese culture that has been adapted to the twentieth-century urban environment.

The Obon Festival has been observed annually in Japan on July 13, 14 and 15, by Buddhist families ever since the introduction of the faith, nearly 2,500 years ago. A main part of the ritual involves a pilgrimage to the graveyard to pay homage to family ancestors. As darkness sets in, every family lights paper lanterns, slowly illuminating the quiet cemetery. Later, it is customary to visit the local temple where the lanterns are often hung in rows like so many rice-paper light bulbs. The Obon Festival created walls of light at a scale that dwarfed human beings centuries before Thomas Edison even began the famous experiments which ultimately led him to discover that a scorched cotton thread could serve as a filament for an incandescent bulb.

Another example of the Japanese fondness for the proliferation of light can be seen at the Kasuga Shrine in Nara, founded in 768, in which 3,000 stone lanterns line both sides of the path to the shrine. These lanterns are lit twice every year on the nights of the Mandoro Festival in February and August. By reinterpreting ancient traditions using contemporary materials and methods, the Japanese have been able to maintain a social stability while making enormous strides in industrial growth. Their facility in employing electrographic architecture to structure their cities is, in fact, the Obon Festival reincarnated in Western attire.

The energy crisis, which hit Japan harder than most of the industrialized world in late 1973 and 1974, may have dimmed some of the bright projections for indus-

312

312, 313.
Sony® Building, Yoshinobu Ashihara, 1966: A vertical shaft of changing patterns provides movement, light and visual richness for this Ginza landmark, which is an equally successful work of architecture during the busy daylight hours.
314–316.
Kinetic Cornice, Nippon Electric Company, Ginza District, Tokyo: The computerized light show covering the upper portion of Tokyo office towers produces the electrographic, Kinetic Cornice, a plugged-in, turned-on, modern-day evolution of the classic order.

trial growth forecast in the early seventies; but it did not stem the tide of innovation, nor did it change that country's commitment to expanded technological advancement. Some of the kinetic cornices may have been turned on for shorter periods, and the supply of oil to residences was drastically curtailed, but the electrographic city did not go out. It continued to glow and hum with the precision of a finely tuned instrument. In a nation where it is traditional to build without insulation, and where sitting in heavily quilted kimonos with the sliding doors open watching the snow fall peacefully in the garden is considered not only normal, but the height of serenity and joy, the cutback in household fuel was not received with public outcry, but rather with calm complacence. Designing in harmony with nature is traditional to Japan, and the strict economy in energy consumption is not as much of an inconvenience to the Japanese as it might be to Europeans, and definitely is to Americans. The Japanese are currently studying methods to conserve energy in building and should have some valuable contributions to make to this important field in the near future.

313

314

315

316

317.
Kasuga Shrine, Nara, founded in 768: The Japanese fondness for the proliferation of light can be traced to ancient rituals and festivals. At the Kasuga Shrine, 3,000 stone lanterns are lit twice annually to celebrate the Mandoro Festival.

317

Computer City

Computer City is a collection of computer-assisted environments designed to be self-contained, totally enclosed, and independent universes. As early as 1962 Buckminster Fuller proposed a dome two miles (3.2 km) wide and one mile (1.6 km) high at its center to cover a portion of central Manhattan. Fuller later explained that, "There are inexorably persuasive arguments in favour of cities under single umbrella shells."[72] One of Fuller's arguments included the fact that energy conservation increases as the volume of the enclosed city increases.

The Japanese have taken Fuller's arguments to heart and have begun testing the concept of large covered cities through the design and construction of several computer-assisted climatically-controlled environments. One of the most successful of these is the Nagashima Tropical Garden designed and built by Takenaka Komuten in 1968. After the discovery of therapeutic hot springs at Nagashima, about twelve miles (19.2 km) from downtown Nagoya, Takenaka developed this tourist mini-village. Covering 36 acres (14.6 hectares) is a prototypical mass-leisure complex capable of handling 1,600,000 people a year. The enclosure itself is composed of steel space-frame units sheathed in transluscent fiberglass forming a modern-day, plastic Crystal Palace.[73] Within the building, Takenaka has created a series of computer-controlled microclimates in which the visitor may experience a dry desert, lush tropical foliage, or a plantation of ivy and ferns, complete with a community of thatched huts for the imaginary residents. A large variety of fish, fowl, and animal wildlife inhabit the vast enclosure the year round.

318

318.
New York City Dome, Buckminster Fuller, 1962: An early radical proposal by Bucky for covering large areas of cities to provide a computer-controlled, energy-efficient environment.

319, 320.
Nagashima Tropical Garden, Takenaka Komuten Co., Ltd., 1968: A prototypical mass-leisure complex composed of steel trusses and a transluscent fiberglass skin, creating a modern-day Crystal Palace. Computer-controlled microclimates recreate environments from throughout the world.

320

Similar sprawling mass-leisure complexes are being built outside many of Japan's dense urban centers. Kisho Kurokawa designed the Yamagata Hawaii Dreamland, the first increment of which is complete. Thirty minutes from Tokyo's Shinjuku Station is Summerland. Designed by Kinji Fumada, Minoru Murakami and Toshio Sato as another computer-controlled city, this leisure complex sits in the rural landscape like a surreal, interplanetary visitor. Inside the translucent, truncated enclosure, tropical gardens and large swimming pools with fully mechanized waves and ocean spray mimic the natural wonders of the South Pacific.

A cohesive, conformist society, the people of Japan are accustomed to high density in all aspects of living, whether involving work or play. These expansive pleasure palaces allow the citizens of an urban society the opportunity to escape the harsh realities of the city for a technological, prefabricated imitation of nature that is unavailable to most in its orginal state. Oiso Long Beach, just outside Tokyo, is made up of six different lakes and pools including one that is 600 m (nearly 2,000 ft) long with a continuous circular tide that gently glides its visitors around on floating islands.

Within the city itself Takenaka Komuten has completed the first Newtown-in-town devoted solely to entertainment, sports,

321

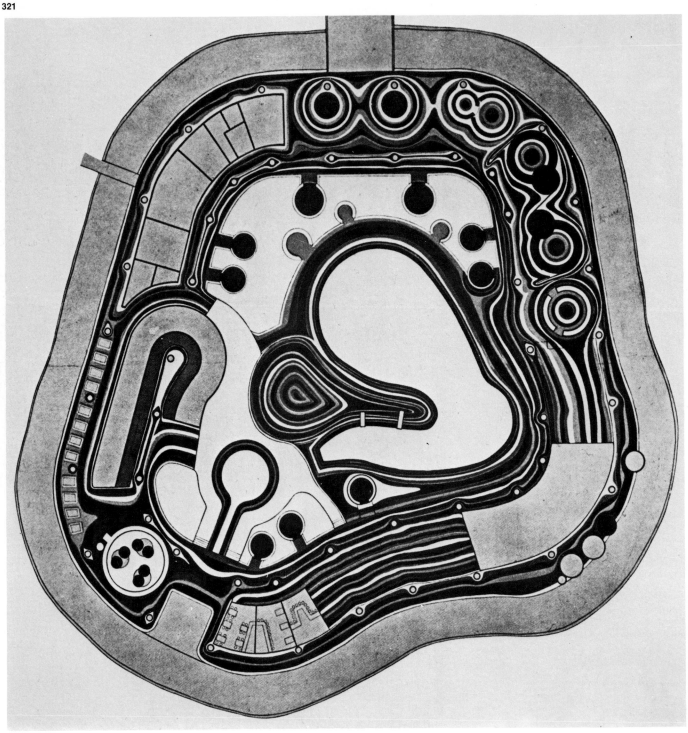

and amusement. The focus of this new entertainment environment is the Korakuen Yellow Building completed in 1973. Located amid a huge sports complex, with the famous Korakuen Gardens nearby, the area is renowned as an amusement center. The brightly colored lemon-yellow and orange structure includes an artificial land platform, the Plaza of the Sun, which contains the 100-foot-high (30 m) zelkova trees unique to this locale. Adjacent to the

321.
Yamagata Hawaii Dreamland, Kisho Kurokawa, 1967: Conceived as a computerized, escapist fantasy, Kurokawa has clustered together a hot spring, public baths, bowling alleys, an aquarium, and a variety of other leisure facilities.

322, 323.
Summerland; Fumaka, Murakami and Sato, 1967: A futurist pleasure-palace of mechanized waves and ocean spray recreates the wonders of the South Pacific.

324.
Oiso Long Beach: Another mega-resort where technology blurs individual identity. This water wonderland contains six different pools and ponds, including this 600-meter (2,000-ft) pool complete with a mechanized tide that floats its occupants along, past the rows of sunbathers. (See figure 161.)

322

323

324

plaza is the glass-enclosed circulation tower—five stories of interlocking escalators, stairs and elevators—unifying the entire multistory complex into a single urban pleasure palace. Within the complex itself are bowling alleys, ice skating rinks, cafes, restaurants, and pools. Against the pallid, urban landscape of Tokyo this polychromatic wonderland enhances nature and restores what is lacking in our cities—a sense of wonder, color, and joy.

Unlike the United States, whose entertainment environments such as Disneyland, Magic Mountain, or Disney World can be spread across vast, barren landscape, Japan has been forced to create amusement centers within very limited areas. This has given rise to the totally enclosed, climatically-controlled amusement centers which are manifesting themselves throughout Japan.

A more ambitious application of a Computer City is the Post University Pack of Arata Isozaki. It is an urban nucleus, included in which is: a hospital complex, a laboratory complex, an office complex, a local community center, a shopping center, and a convention hall. Everything is packaged in one envelope. There is both a mass transit and personal transit system. The roof is a continuous membrane similar to the one envisioned by Buckminster Fuller for New York City. Isozaki explained that, "This is a conceptual model of life

325

325–327.
Korakuen Yellow Building, Takenaka Komuten Co., Ltd., 1973: Part of a vast amusement complex, this miniature leisure city provides a supergraphic escapist environment in contrast to the harsh reality of urban Tokyo. (See color plate 186.)
328–330.
Post University Pack, Computer City, Arata Isozaki, 1972: Part of Isozaki's continuing study of computer-generated models, systems analysis and technological innovation. The long tubular enclosures form the linear town center. When viewed in section (330), the membrane enclosure is reminiscent of the dome Bucky Fuller proposed for New York City (318). The Energy Network (329) links the neighborhood clusters with energy generators.

326

327

where all city center activities are 'packed' into one environment in order to learn something, so I call this, 'after the university' or 'Post University Pack'." Using a systems-analysis approach to the problem of designing a new town, Isozaki takes into account various service networks such as the school system, the library system, the pollution control system, the medical services system, etc. From these he classified three basic city systems: control, service, and information. Out of this research Isozaki developed a network called the "Wired City System." The Wired City System and the Post University Pack form part of the research Isozaki has been conducting in the design of Kaihin New Town for Chiba Prefecture across the bay from Tokyo. Although still in the conceptual phase, the success of the Japanese Computer City models which have been built as pleasure domes, indicates that a Wired City New Town is not very far from reality.

328

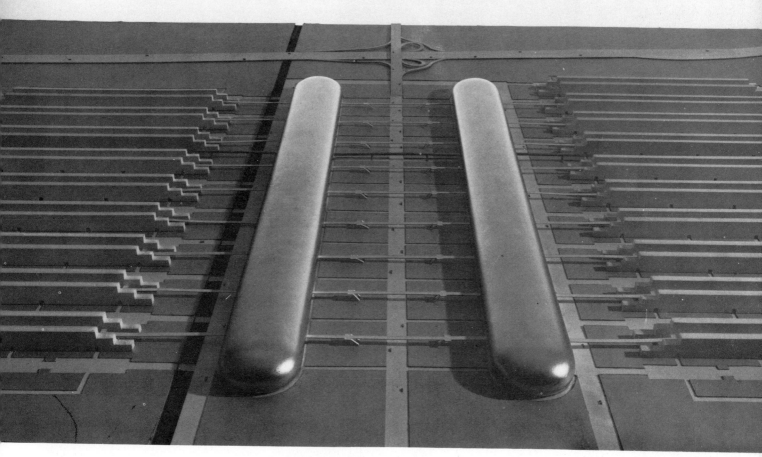

329

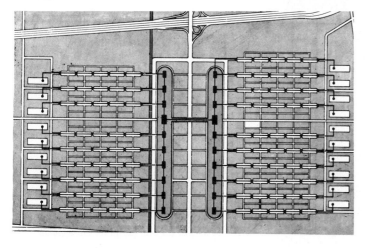

330

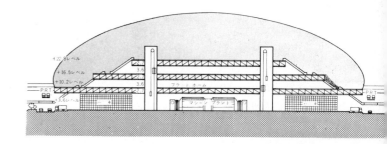

Inflatable City

Symbolic of Japan's interest in inflatable technology is the "Moving Hand" sculpture by Shiro Takanashi which welcomed visitors to the computer-art exhibit, called Cybernetic Artrip, held appropriately in the progressive Sony® Building. The Moving Hand motioned people in like the *maneki-neko,* or beckoning cat, popular in Japanese commercial establishments. The hand was also programmed to create several traditional Buddhist *mudra,* or hand gestures, symbolizing eternal peace and tranquility in a changing world. This kinetic sculpture reflecting ancient religious gestures is part of the Both/And culture of Japan that helped produce the innovative approach to architectural design of Yutaka Murata.

An inflatable city has been the long-term goal of Japan's foremost architect of pneumatic structures, Yutaka Murata. At a lecture delivered at the International Symposium on Pneumatic Structures in Delft, The Netherlands, at which Murata was the guest speaker, he explained that, "From the first phase of the development of pneumatic theory, there have been predictions that the pneumatic structure could be developed into a megastructure capable of becoming an urban or regional envelope. Today it is quite possible to realize such enormous structures."[74] A firm believer in the potential of pneumatic structures, Murata has been persevering for many years in the pursuit of an inflatable city.

331

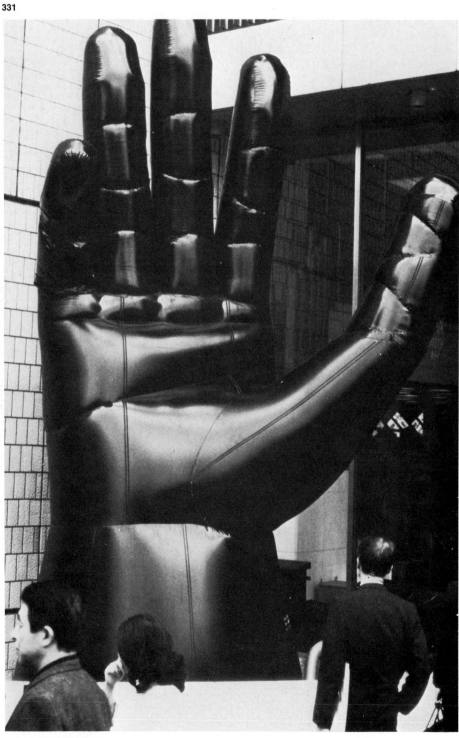

332

His imagination first captured the attention of the architectural world with the extraordinary Fuji Group Pavilion at Expo '70 in Osaka. One of several pneumatic structures he designed for Expo '70, the Fuji Group Pavilion was distinguished from the United States Pavilion in that it was an "air-inflated" structure, whereas the American pavilion was of the "air-supported" type. The structure of the Fuji Group Pavilion, designed by Murata in conjunction with Dr. Mamoru Kawaguchi, is called air-inflated because it is composed of 16 air-inflated arches 4 m (13 ft) in diameter and 72 m (236 ft) in length. The structural members themselves were made of polyvinyl alcohol fiber canvas. A similar, but smaller pavilion at Expo '70 was the Floating Theater of the Electric Power Company also designed by Murata.

An interesting feature of the Fuji Pavilion was the inclusion of several mini-pneumatic structures within the 100-foot-high (30 m) volume. These diminutive versions of the pavilion itself included an information tent, a cafe, and an inflatable washroom. This concept of putting one pneumatic structure within another, Murata believes, is the key to a much broader use of this new technology. He has pointed out that, "It was quite apparent from the early stages of its development that the greatest potential of the pneumatic structure lay in its use on a gigantic scale, and in relation with this possibility, there should naturally arise another possibility inside the envelope: 'pneumatic in pneumatic'."[75]

333

334

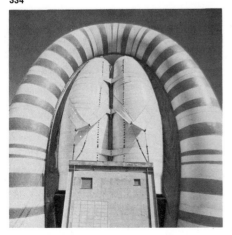

335

331, 332.
Moving Hand, Shiro Takanashi, 1973: This kinetic sculpture welcomed visitors to a computer art exhibit called Cybernetic Artrip®, held appropriately in the Tokyo Sony® Building. It represents the Japanese artist's unbending interest in new technology in general, and in inflatable structures in particular.

333, 334.
Fuji Group Pavilion, Expo '70, Yutaka Murata, 1970: The strongest protagonist of pneumatic structures in Japan, Murata first captured the attention of the architectural world with this ribbed, air-inflated pavilion.

335.
Floating Theater, Electrical Power Pavilion, Expo '70, Yutaka Murata, 1970: Three large tubes, 3 meters (10 ft) in diameter and 40 meters (125 ft) in length, support this amphibious, polyester, canvas structure.

Murata envisions vast pneumatic skins stretched over new communities to be erected in remote parts of the world where construction technology is limited and where building materials are few. These membrane-covered new communities would be similar to the City in the Arctic project proposed by Frei Otto and Atelier Warmbronn in association with Kenzo Tange & URTEC,[76] but with several key refinements. Within this thick-skinned city, lightweight fiber substructures could be erected which need not be fortified against the external loads of wind, rain,

and snow. These polypneumatic substructures Murata has labeled "pneumatic in pneumatic."

The first of several proposals employing this principle is Murata's Pneumatic Poly-Climate Pavilion. Made up of four intersecting air-supported domes, the 180,000-sq ft (16,500-m²) structure is enclosed by a transparent double membrane. Each of the four spaces has different climatic zones separated by a transparent wall composed of a three-layer mylar membrane. Each layer contains an air space

which insulates the different zones and prevents condensation on the winter surface. A person enjoying the warmth of summer bathing in one zone may vicariously experience the vigor of winter ice skating in the adjacent space.

The center of the complex contains the heat-exchange unit. This energy-efficient system takes the heat gained by the pumps from refrigerating the ice-skating rinks and transfers it to the zones containing the swimming pools.

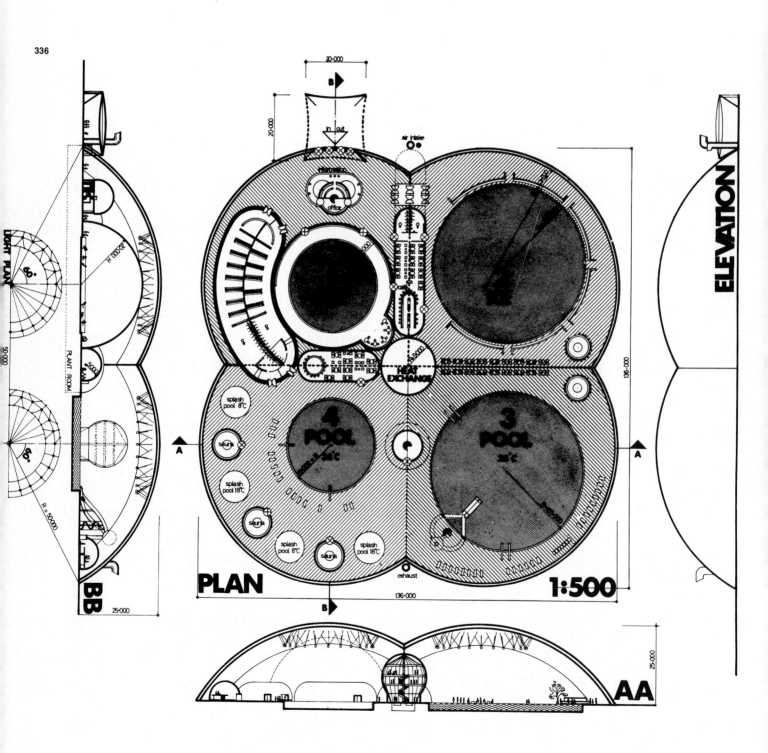

336

The external envelope is printed with electrically heated metal strands which prevent deformation of the structure from heavy snow loads, much the way rear window defrosters work in automobiles. Glass fiber is hung from the inner membrane for fire protection and to reduce the reverberation within the domes. Generally speaking, Murata has gone to great lengths to consider all the possible situations the structure may be exposed to and has designed a solution that works and can be easily constructed using contemporary technology.

337

336, 337.
Pneumatic Poly-Climate Pavilion, Yutaka Murata, 1973: Four adjacent air-supported domes enclose a variety of poly-pneumatic environments of greatly differing temperatures and requirements.

Within this polyclimatic pavilion he has created a series of minipneumatic environments, achieving once again his goal of "pneumatic in pneumatic." These include a torus-shaped locker room, a children's ice-skating rink, a variety of saunas and splash pools, an administrative office, and a centrally located cafe from which one can view all four climatic zones. Each space is supplied with the temperature, humidity, and air pressure appropriate to its function.

At the request of the Soviet Union, Murata has also been investigating the potential of inflatable cities for Siberia, where construction time is limited to three summer months. To date he has designed a sports complex/convention center and a 1-km-long (3,280-ft) recreational park. The sports complex/convention center is composed of several structures containing assembly spaces, bowling alleys, basketball courts, and volleyball courts. The one-kilometer park is based on the concept of

New York's Central Park by Frederick Law Olmstead, in which the park forms the nucleus of a larger, dense, residential community. Murata's park typically contains a diversity of outdoor recreational activities including bicycle paths; tennis, volleyball and basketball courts; a senior citizens' labyrinth for quiet strolls; and, of course, bathing and ice-skating zones within their own pneumatic enclosures. Based on a grid of 100 m (328 ft), what appear to be columns in the plan are ac-

338

339

338.
Sports Complex, Yutaka Murata, 1972: Prepared as one of several structures for the Soviet Union, which has long winters and brief periods for conventional construction in their frigid northeast Siberian region.
339.
Fuyo Group Pavilion, Expo '75, Yutaka Murata, 1975: A torus-shaped inflatable gallery is integrated with bold space frames and a cable-net tensile structure.
340, 341.
One Kilometer Park, Yutaka Murata, 1972: Also prepared at the request of the Soviet Union, this inflatable city contains a marina, cafes, sports facilities and vast parklands for bicycling, strolling and other "outdoor" activities.

tually roof drains which structurally serve to tie down the membrane rather than support it.

For Japan's Ocean Expo '75 in Okinawa, Murata was again commissioned by the Fuyo Group to design a multipurpose pavilion, part of which would remain at the conclusion of the exposition. The pavilion consists of three major elements: (1) the pergola, a cable-net tension roof, (2) the central pavilion itself composed of a torus-shaped gallery and a domed auditorium (both pneumatic structures), and (3) the administrative offices, which are made up of fiber-reinforced polyester cupolas. The pergola, with its double, cable-net roof supported by six space-frame pillars has remained for open-air concerts after the end of the exposition. Continuing to test this new technology against different environments and internal functions, Murata still looks toward the day when he will be commissioned to create a complete inflatable city.

340

391

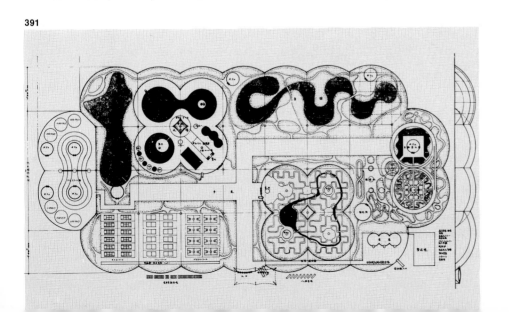

Floating City

During a period spanning two decades, Kiyonori Kikutake has been engaged in the design of a variety of floating cities. More fortunate than other visionary architects, Kikutake saw a major part of his vision realized in Okinawa during the summer of Expo '75. The Japanese Government presented the exhibit as a prototype of the floating city of the future, calling it Aquapolis—an aquatic acropolis. A massive pavilion reminiscent of the earlier Metabolist megastructures, the Aquapolis stands 60 ft (18 m) above the water and occupies an area of 2.5 acres (10,000 m²). The floating city is designed to submerge itself 50 ft (15 m) into the ocean during inclement weather by pumping water into or out of the lower hull. Even during storms the Aquapolis is purported to list only one degree.

The colossal construction of columns, tubes, and platforms contains an exhibition hall, conference room, living capsule, sea-water conversion apparatus, the Aquapolis cockpit, and a large assortment of other devices and mechanisms for maintaining life, including its own sewage-disposal system.

For an island nation with crowded cities and limited resources the notion of being able to expand out onto the ocean's surface and below its depths has been a long-standing dream of several Japanese architects. Kenzo Tange first proposed a floating city in Tokyo Bay in his Plan for Tokyo 1960. This was followed by projects of equal buoyancy by Kisho Kurokawa, Kiyonori Kikutake, Shoji Sadao and others;

342.
Marina City, Kiyonori Kikutake, 1958: Clearly influenced by Chicago's Marina City towers designed by Bertrand Goldberg, which had been published in model form. These seminal sketches proposed vast artificial land platforms linking together cylindrical structures.
343.
Ocean City, Kiyonori Kikutake, 1963: A further refinement of the Metabolist schemes Kikutake proposed in 1961. (See figure 44.)
344, 345.
Marine Exposition, Hawaii, Kiyonori Kikutake and Hugh Burgess, 1971: The most realistic floating city as of that date, this scheme included tensile structure, tent-covered communities, a circular monorail, and facilities for helicopter and hydrofoil.
346.
Preliminary Model, Aquapolis, Kiyonori Kikutake, 1973: This simplified model was the basis for the final scheme which seems to merge Tange's Yamanashi Communications Center with off-shore drilling platforms, symbols of the voracious energy appetite of the industrial world.
347–349.
Aquapolis, Expo '75, Okinawa, Kiyonori Kikutake and Mitsubishi® Heavy Industries, 1975: Off-shore from the International Exposition, this fabulous floating city contains its own power generators, sewage disposal system, and sea-water converter apparatus.

342

343

344

345
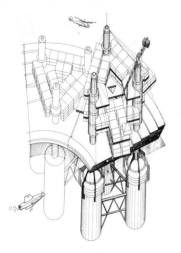

346

but by far the most persevering and indefatigable of the floating city enthusiasts was Kikutake. As early as 1958 Kikutake produced several crude yet prophetic sketches of large, donut-shaped clusters, which were the beginning of a long series of marina-city proposals. These rough sketches led to Ocean City 1961 which called for cylindrical towers set on floating circular base pads. In 1963 Kikutake produced another version; this time he simplified the scheme to cylindrical towers growing directly out of the ocean. In 1970 he was invited to Hawaii to participate in the design of a Marine Exposition with the University of Hawaii marine studies department. Along with Hugh Burgess, AIA, Kikutake produced, in 1971, his most realistic and ambitious floating city proposal. It included a hotel, dormitory, apartments, commercial facilities, office space, a research center, and an exhibition area—all of which were integrated into a vast circular harbor. The city contained an internal monorail, a wave damping system, and a hydrofoil entrance and exit for quick commutes to the adjacent islands. The in-depth research conducted by the team as a whole made the very notion of a floating city all the more plausible. By 1973 Kikutake was back in Japan working on a simplified rectangular volume supported by cylindrical cores set in the ocean. These preliminary models of the final solution seem to merge the Metabolist technology of Tange's Yamanashi Communications Center with the off-shore industrial oil-drilling rigs which emerged out of the sea in the second half of this century. The Aquapolis itself sits 400 m (1300 ft) off the Motobu Peninsula, floating quietly into the future.

347

348

349

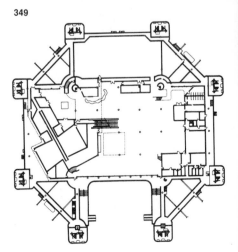

Movable City and Instant City

In 1964 Ron Herron of Archigram produced a futurist montage called Walking City, in which several mobile super-containers lumbered along on telescoping legs and wheeled feet. The futurist fantasy proved too cumbersome even for New York, upon which the montage was superimposed, and the walking pods wandered off to take their proper place amid the unbuilt dreams of the sixties. Archigram later proposed the euphoric Instant City of tent structures suspended from balloons. The concepts of movability

and flexibility within the urban fabric as promulgated by these schemes, which prompted token imitation throughout the world until the balloons burst, have actually been practiced in Japan for centuries and are presently being realized on practically a daily basis at local *matsuri* (festivals) in every prefecture in the country.

Instant City is, in effect, a Movable City which relocates and reappears so quickly it gives the illusion of being instantaneous. A nation seasoned in the ephemeral architecture of interchangeable com-

350

350–352.
Instant City as Movable City: Throughout Japan, mini-cafes and restaurants cluster together after dark to form nocturnal nodes in the urban fabric. The storefront seen by day (350) attracts patrons to the *oden* and *soba* stands, which gather in the evening near a subway exit (351, 352).

ponents, Japan has developed a mobile architecture, elements of which appear at regular intervals and in certain locations, transforming a given environment into a totally different place. In front of railway stations and grocery stores or at any locus of human activity, a cluster of street vendors will collect, forming a subcenter within the city which is inhabited by a group of individuals forming a community. Each vendor fashions his minishop to create the effect of a small building. A diminutive pitched roof with the traditional *noren* (shop curtain) and a few light stools which have been transported for the occasion, are enough to simulate a small restaurant. Huddled over the hot *soba* (noodles) or traditional *oden* (stew) the customers exchange pleasantries and chat with the vendor every evening on their way home from work. Within the confines of these mobile cafes one feels himself to be in a miniature village or city. These instant cities appear each evening as the stores close and the skies turn dark, but have disappeared by morning as one enters the same subway station on his way to work. The vendors represent a rare mixture of flexibility and continuity. As the cities grow and neighborhoods change the mobile street vendors relocate, set up shop, and before long the nocturnal instant cities have retrenched and become almost permanent fixtures. The frequent customers become regulars and new patterns become old as the instant city is continually reborn.

These vendors travel the paths of the most urban sections of Tokyo selling the staples of the society, each with his own music or song to attract his clientele. The familiar sound of the soba-vendors' flute-like instrument, the *charumela,* is followed by the melodic invitation of the man

351

352

ing hot, baked sweet potatoes on cold winter nights. Each season has its specialists. In the spring there appears a veritable tropical fish store on wheels, with its racks of glass fish bowls and shiny gold fish reflecting the lights of the city. Another day will bring the man selling long poles for hanging laundry (traditionally made of bamboo, today transformed into blue plastic); or a complete fruit and vegetable store on wheels; or perhaps nothing more than the *tofu* (soy bean curd) peddler, whose wares are bought daily to assure

freshness. These descendants of traditional Japan recreate instant cities amid the asphalt and concrete wherever people gather together to socialize and purchase their products.

As regular as the daily visit of the street vendor are the religious festivals which occur annually, monthly, or at some other predetermined date which hasn't changed for more than a thousand years. The passive, tranquil temples and shrines which are pockets of repose within the tumul-

tuous city, at regular intervals become transformed into village bazaars and shopping arcades. The simple treelined paths fill with tent structures selling everything from food to religious poems, and then without warning, the instant city vanishes and the quiet religious order returns. This apparent contradiction or paradox is nothing more than a contemporary continuation of a flexibility and adaptability to change that has long since become a basic part of the Japanese Both/And culture. Physical environments or material

353

354

353–356.
Matsuri Instant City, Tokyo: The serene temple gardens (353, 355), which serve as a quiet refuge for meditation and peace from the city's noise and intensity, are themselves transformed into village bazaars and communal meeting places in celebration of ritual religious *matsuri* (festivals) (354, 356).
357.
Street Vendor, Tokyo: Maintaining an ancient Japanese tradition, this vendor is selling poles for hanging out wet *kimono* and other laundry. Contemporary society has seen the long bamboo poles of old evolve into blue plastic, and the vendor's melodic voice becomes amplified with a battery-operated megaphone. This is but one manifestation of the flexible, adaptable Both/And culture of Japan.

355

356

objects that are bestowed with great inner meaning on one day can be discarded, forgotten, and replaced with new objects or environments having equal meaning and value. The venerable Ise Shrine is annually lavished with symbolic value as hundreds of thousands of people make their pilgrimage on New Year's Day; yet, every 20 years these highly esteemed structures are razed and replaced with new ones on an adjacent plot to be revered and respected just as much as those which were destroyed the previous year.

This is the secret of the Both/And culture; that it can revere the past, yet discard it for the future; that it can create fantasies without losing touch with utter reality; and that it can pursue new directions, yet remain on a steady course.

If Instant City, Inflatable City, Floating City, and Electrographic City represent potential urban alternatives for the environments of the future, then I believe we can safely say that in Japan the future is now.

357

Notes

General Note
Selected portions of this manuscript have been previously published by *Architecture Plus,* May-June 1974; *A+U, A Monthly Journal of World Architecture and Urbanism, June, 1976;* and by *Environmental Communications,*® Venice, California. All statements by persons quoted in this book that are not noted were made either during personal interviews or in correspondence to the author.

1
Alvin Toffler, *Future Shock,* Bantam Books, Inc., New York, 1970, p. 189.

2
Ibid, p. 195.

3
According to the December 19, 1976 *Los Angeles Times,* "Honda automobile sales in the United States have more than tripled since 1974. . . . The Company, which did not sell automobiles here before 1971, is now the fourth largest importer and it topped sales of No. 3 Volkswagen during October." (Of course, the No. 1 and No. 2 spots are shared by Toyota and Datsun.)

The Honda Civic, introduced in 1974, and the Accord, introduced here in 1976, both have the advanced CVCC engine. Several 1977 models recorded better than 50 mpg in the EPA simulated highway driving tests. Good mileage, combined with dependability and over-all economy have given the Japanese the edge.

Mazda Motor Company bought the rights to develop the rotary engine from Wankel, the original designer, and are producing the advanced engine for commercial consumption.

4
Herman Kahn, *The Emerging Japanese Superstate,* Prentice Hall, Inc., Englewood Cliffs, N.J., 1970, p. 8.

5
Noboru Kawazoe, "From Metabolism to Metapolis—Proposal for a City of the Future," in *Urban Structures for the Future,* by Justus Dahinden, Praeger Publishers, New York, 1972, p. 205.

6
Ruth Benedict, *The Chrysanthemum and the Sword,* The World Publishing Company, Cleveland and New York, 1946, p. 2.

7
Robert Venturi, *Complexity and Contradiction in Architecture,* The Museum of Modern Art, New York, 1966, p. 31.

8
Jesse Kuhaulua and John Wheeler, *Takamiyama, the World of Sumo,* Kodansha International, Tokyo, 1973, p. 28.

9
Noboru Kawazoe, *Contemporary Japanese Architecture,* The Japan Foundation, Tokyo, Japan, 1973, p. 19.

10
Antonin Raymond, From a conversation with the author, January 13, 1973, Azabu, Tokyo.

11
Arthur Drexler, *The Architecture of Japan,* The Museum of Modern Art, New York, 1955, p. 242.

12
See Noboru Kawazoe, *Contemporary Japanese Architecture,* p. 21

13
Kawazoe, *Contemporary Japanese Architecture,* p. 21.

14
In feudal Japan it was customary for whole families to participate in a craft or business, and for the skill to be handed down from one generation to the next. This custom permeated the entire culture. There were families who specialized in ceramics, or kite making, or in making lanterns or in making the traditional Samurai sword. Many of these highly skilled craftsmen were considered fine artists in their day and each taught the secrets of his craft to his son in order to carry on the family tradition.

One of the most highly prized artisans was the *daiku* or carpenter. In Japanese *dai* literally means "great" and *ku* means "craft," "art," or "artisan." Thus a carpenter family was a rare family of "great artisans," skilled in the design, engineering and construction of Japan's complex, bracketed wooden architecture.

15
For a more detailed discussion of the far-reaching implications of the master-disciple structure, see *Japanese Society* by Chie Nakane, Penguin Books Ltd., Harmondsworth, Middx., 1970, pp. 61–62.

16
Architectural Forum, March 1952.

17
For a detailed account of the fascinating career of Mr. Raymond, see, *Antonin Raymond, An Autobiography,* Charles E. Tuttle Company, Rutland, Vermont and Tokyo, 1973.

18
Drexler, *The Architecture of Japan,* p. 247.

19
Kawazoe, *Contemporary Japanese Architecture,* p. 28.

20
Kawazoe, Ibid., p. 30.

21
Derived from the words "Urbanist Architect"; it is the name of Tange's firm.

22
Kenzo Tange, From *The Japan Architect,* reprinted in *Investigations in Collective Form* by Fumihiko Maki, The School of Architecture, Washington University, St. Louis, 1964, p. 11.

23
Kenzo Tange, *The Japan Architect,* September, 1971, p. 29.

24
Fumihiko Maki and Masato Otaka, "Some Thoughts on Collective Form," *Metabolism 1960,* Bijutsu Shuppan-sha Tokyo, 1960. Republished in, *Structure In Art And In Science,* edited by Gyorgy Kepes, George Braziller, Inc., New York 1965, p. 120.

25
See Chapter 5: *Futurism: Floating City,* for a more comprehensive review of Kikutake's Marina City Development.

26
Archigram is the name taken by an avantegarde group of British architects and urban designers which developed in the early 1960s. Their proposed technological urban structures, such as Peter Cook's Plug-in City, Ron Herron's Walking City, Warren Chalk's Capsule Homes Tower, and Dennis Crompton's Computer City, had a profound effect on the development of the megastructure concept in Japan. (See Chapter 3, Architechnology p. 55).

27
Kenzo Tange, *The Japan Architect,* January, 1967, p. 28.

28
Reyner Banham, *Megastructure, Urban Futures of the Recent Past,* Harper and Row, Publishers, Inc., New York, 1976, p. 7.

29
Robert Venturi and Denise Scott Brown, "Ugly and Ordinary Architecture or the Decorated Shed," *The Architectural Forum,* December 1971, p. 52.

30
Jonathan Barnett, *Urban Design as Public Pol-*

icy, Architectural Record Books, New York, 1974, p. 4.

31
Banham, *Megastructure, Urban Futures of the Recent Past*, p. 11.

32
The Japan Times, April 22, 1973, p. 8.

33
Herman Kahn, *The Emerging Japanese Superstate,* Prentice-Hall Inc., Englewood Cliffs, N.J., 1970, p. 8.

34
Bernard Rudofsky, *The Kimono Mind,* Charles E. Tuttle Co., Tokyo, 1971, p. 259.

35
Alvin Toffler, *Future Shock,* p. 60.

36
See Chapter 2. *Megastructuring,* for a more detailed discussion of the Pilot House and the Ashiyahama Housing Competitions.

37
Yoshichika Uchida, "Industrialized Buildings and Modular Co-ordination," *Glass and Architecture,* February 1971, p. 4.

38
Toffler, *Future Shock,* p. 267.

39
Marshall McLuhan and George B. Leonard, "The Future of Education," *Look,* February 21, 1967, p. 23.

40
Misawa Homes Institute of Research and Development, Technical Report, Vol. 13, p. 1.

41
Toffler, *Future Shock,* p. 266.

42
Akira Shibuya of GAUS is the same architect who won *The Japan Architect* housing competition of 1966 described in Chapter 2, *Megastructuring.*

43
Toffler, *Future Shock,* p. 222.

44
See the interesting book from the exhibit: Susan King, "The Drawings of Eric Mendelsohn," University of California, Berkeley, 1969.

45
Bruno Zevi, *Architecture As Space,* Horizon Press, New York, 1975.

46
Wylie Sypher, *Four Stages of Renaissance Style,* Doubleday & Company, Inc., Garden City, New York, 1955, p. 70.

47
Hugo Munsterberg, *The Arts of Japan,* Charles E. Tuttle Company, Tokyo, 1957, p. 113.

48
Fumihiko Maki, *Investigations In Collective Form,* the School of Architecture, Washington University, St. Louis, p. 6.

49
Fumihiko Maki and Masato Otaka, "Some Thoughts on Collective Form," *Metabolism 1960,* Bijutsu-Shuppan-sha Tokyo, Japan, 1960. Republished in *Structure in Art and in Science,* edited by Gyorgy Kepes, George Braziller, Inc., New York, 1965, p. 116.

50
The term "contextualism" is generally used in reference to physical context, but may also include a reference to cultural context, which is especially true in the work of Fumihiko Maki. The terminology and its implications are discussed in the definitive article by Stuart Cohen, "Physical Context/Cultural Context: Including it All," *Oppositions 2,* The Institute for Architecture and Urban Studies, January 1974.

51
Reyner Banham, *Theory and Design in the First Machine Age,* Praeger Publishers, New York, 1960, p. 329. Part of the concluding paragraph of the book as quoted by Maki in, "At The Beginning of the Last Quarter of The Century, Reflections of a Japanese Architect," *The Japan Architect,* April 1975, p. 20.

52
Bruno Zevi, *Architecture As Space.*

53
The term *pilotis* is used in architecture to refer to rows of freestanding columns at the base or ground plane of a building, which support the entire mass of the structure. This concept, advocated by Le Corbusier in the 1930s, was employed to free the area of the building at the ground for parks and public open spaces. While it made sense for high-rise apartments in suburban areas, such as the Unite d'Habitation at Marseilles by Le Corbusier, it has been imitated widely with less success in dense urban areas. Maki's approach of creating semi-enclosed public open space by using solid surfaces and layers of transparency is more appropriate on a dense urban site adjacent to a busy street.

54
Tanaka, Kakuci, *Building a New Japan: A Plan for Remodelling the Japanese Archipelago,* Simul Press, Tokyo, Japan, 1973.

55
Frampton, Kenneth, "Maison de Verre," *Perspecta 12,* Yale University, New Haven, 1969, p. 80.

56
Wylie Sypher, *Four Stages of Renaissance Style, p. 33.*

57
Peter Cook, *A+U, A Monthly Journal of World Architecture and Urbanism,* 72:01, p. 84.

58
Sypher, *Four Stages of Renaissance Style,* p. 123.

59
For a more detailed analysis of the work and philosophy of ArchiteXt, see Charles Jencks', "ArchiteXt and the Problem of Symbolism," *The Japan Architect,* June 1976, pp. 21–28. (Note: Pages 29 through 80 are devoted to the work of these five radical designers.)

60
Archizoom is an Italian spin-off of the English-based, avante-garde architectural group called Archigram (see Note 27). The name Archizoom is in direct emulation of the work of Archigram which they have studied and admired. The suffixes themselves are satirical comments on the profession of architecture; Archigram originated as a series of architectural telegrams; Archizoom implied a space age, futurist architecture; and ArchiteXt is just another parody on the current vogue in architecture of various "texts" or readings such as "contextualism."

61
Shin'ichi Okada, *The Japan Architect,* January 1973, p. 26.

62
Louis I. Kahn, Address to the Boston Society of Architects, Massachusetts Institute of Technology, Cambridge, Mass., 1966.

63
Shin'ichi Okada, *The Japan Architect,* October 1974, p. 42.

64
Ibid, p. 42.

65
The term *parti* in architecture refers to the basic conceptual approach employed in a design. At the nucleus of every work of architecture is an essential organizing idea from which the final design is evolved. This is called the *parti.* In the case of Okada's Supreme Court Building, the parti was to employ massive space-walls in a parallel series of shifted layers. The final building never developed beyond this simple diagram.

66
Okada, *The Japan Architect,* p. 42.

67
Benedict, *The Chrysanthemum and the Sword,* p. 1.

68
Rudofsky, *The Kimono Mind,* p. 59.

Sources of Illustrations

69
Le Corbusier, *Towards A New Architecture,* Architectural Press, London, 1927, p. 3.
70
David Crane, "The City Symbolic," *Journal of the American Institute of Planners,* November 1960, p. 284.
71
Pachinko parlors are one of the most popular forms of escape and relaxation in Japan. Composed of rows of Pachinko machines (which resemble vertical pin-ball machines), the patrons of Pachinko parlors twirl the shiny silver pellets (1 cm [0.4 in] in diameter) to the top of the machine and watch and listen as they bounce, bing and bong their way into different grooves, slots and holes. Like pin-ball, the entire object of the game is simply to win another game and send more silver balls bouncing along their way. It is purely a game of chance; however, when several hundred machines are lined up in one room, the total sound of the innumerable bouncing balls gives a person a sense of communality without ever losing his own total individuality.
72
Richard Buckminster Fuller, "Design Science-Engineering, an Economic Success of all Humanity," Excerpt from a lecture held in Tel-Aviv in December 1967.
73
The Crystal Palace opened in London in 1851, heralding the beginning of a long history of great international expositions. The building itself was a miracle of the industrial technology of its day. It was a vast hall enclosing 800,000 sq ft (74,350 m²) in plate glass and iron trusswork. It was the beginning of the curtain-walled and membrane-enclosed glass skyscrapers of modern architecture.
74
Yutaka Murata, Excerpt from a lecture, "Future Applications of Pneumatic Structures," given at The International Symposium on Pneumatic Structures, Delft, The Netherlands, September 20–22, 1972.
75
Ibid.
76
See: Thomas Herzog, *Pneumatic Structures, A Handbook of Inflatable Architecture,* Oxford University Press, New York, 1976, p. 115.

Photographs by the Author except as noted below.

Archigram Architects 94, 96; Masao Arai 307; Masao Arai, courtesy Fumihiko Maki 225, 226; Masao Arai, courtesy Masato Otaka 71–73; courtesy Daika Dream House 163, 164; courtesy Buckminster Fuller 318; Arthur Golding 188, 311; A. H. Han, 3, 5, 150, 151, 236, 237; courtesy Arata Isozaki 35, 36, 38, 239–243, 248, 251, 259–261, 264, 267, 328–330; *The Japan Architect* 347; courtesy Charles Jencks 322, 323; Kawasumi, courtesy Shin'ichi Okada 285, 296, 297; Kawasumi, courtesy Kenzo Tange 28, 31; courtesy Kiyonori Kikutake 44, 85–89, 342–346, 349; courtesy Kisho Kurokawa 41–43, 102, 103, 128, 131, 132, 140, 147, 148, 165, 321; courtesy Fumihiko Maki 45, 169, 199, 203, 204, 208, 209, 213, 215, 218–223, 230–234; Mitsuo Matsuoka 348; courtesy Misawa Homes 122, 123; courtesy Mitsui Construction Company 98, 99; Kaneaki Monma, courtesy Fumihiko Maki 181, 182, 210, 211, 227, 229; Osamu Murai, courtesy Fumihiko Maki 46, 179, 180, 216, 217; Osamu Murai, courtesy Kenzo Tange 33, 34, 90, 93; courtesy Yutaka Murata 333–341; courtesy Tatsuhiko Nakajima & GAUS 97, 152; Taisuke Ogawa, courtesy Fumihiko Maki 228;

Taisuke Ogawa, courtesy Shin'ichi Okada 291, 293, 295; courtesy Ogawa Tent Company 162; Yasuhiro Ogawa, courtesy Fumihiko Maki 198; Tomio Ohashi 112, 114, 118; Tomio Ohashi, courtesy Kisho Kurokawa 53, 54, 57, 105–109, 129, 130, 133, 141–146; Tomio Ohashi, courtesy Shin'ichi Okada 294; courtesy Katsuhiko Ohno 119–121; courtesy Shin'ichi Okada 286, 289, 290; courtesy Masato Otaka 68–70, 74–76; courtesy Sachio Otani 80–82; courtesy Panasonic 300; courtesy Kevin Roche, John Dinkeloo and Associates 273; Tatsuzo Sato 2; courtesy Akira Shibuya 47–52; courtesy Shinihon Steel Company 126; Shinkenchiku-sha, courtesy Arata Isozaki 166, 262, 263, 265, 266, 268, 269; Shinkenchiku-sha, courtesy Fumihiko Maki 214, 224; Shokokusha Publishing Company, courtesy Shin'ichi Okada 287, 288, 292; Shokokusha Publishing Company, courtesy Minoru Takeyama 272, 274, 275, 283; courtesy Sokagakkai 194–197; courtesy Takenaka Komuten 58–64, 186, 325–327; courtesy Minoru Takeyama 185, 187, 270, 276, 277–282, 284; courtesy Kenzo Tange 29, 67, 91, 92; courtesy Yoshichika Uchida 113, 115–117; courtesy Yoji Watanabe 156; Yoshio Watanabe 26.

Index